A
Guide
to the
Campus of
The University
of Michigan

The University

There are few earthly things more beautiful than a University.
It is a place where those who hate ignorance
may strive to know, where those who perceive truth
may strive to make others see; where seekers and learners alike,
banded together in the search for knowledge, will honor thought
in all its finer ways, will welcome thinkers in distress
or in exile, will uphold ever the dignity of thought and learning
and will exact standards in these things.
....
There are few earthly things more splendid than a University.
In these days of broken frontiers and collapsing values,
when the dams are down and the floods are making misery,
when every future looks somewhat grim
and every ancient foothold has become something of a quagmire,
wherever a University stands, it stands and shines;
wherever it exists, the free minds of men,
urged on to full and fair inquiry,
may still bring wisdom into human affairs.

— John Masefield

Reprinted by permission of the Society of Authors as the literary representative of the Estate of John Masefield.

A Guide to the Campus of The University of Michigan

by
Margo MacInnes

with the assistance of Wystan Stevens

The University of Michigan Press
ANN ARBOR

Foreword

More than a century and a half have elapsed since 1817 when The University of Michigan was established in the frontier town of Detroit. Twenty years later the University received a forty-acre gift from a group of local residents and moved to its present location in Ann Arbor. Already cleared of forest, the site consisted of a wheat field, peach orchard, and pasture. At that time some two thousand persons lived in Ann Arbor. Today, this city of more than one hundred thousand residents includes over thirty-five thousand University students. The University campus has grown from the original forty acres to more than twenty-five hundred acres.

Campus buildings are a visible manifestation of the University's threefold mission of teaching, research, and service. University activities extend far beyond the city's borders, ranging from laboratories on campus to the Douglas Lake Biological Station in the northern Lower Peninsula, an astronomy observatory in Arizona, and instruments which have orbited the Earth in research satellites. Poets, historians, designers of bridges and airplanes, inventors of vaccines, and the three-man crew of Apollo XV—all are alumni of The University of Michigan.

The University's academic and physical resources are impressive. Its campuses include over two hundred buildings, of which three, the President's House, Kelsey Museum of Archaeology, and the University Observatory are listed in the National Park Service Register of Historic Places.

In addition to support by the State of Michigan, many of the buildings on the three campuses are a result of the generosity of friends and alumni of the University. Some of these buildings are of great architectural interest. Others provide utilitarian space without pretending to be of lasting architectural value. But all serve to fulfill the University's threefold mission.

The hope is that this *Guidebook* to the campuses will make a visit to The University of Michigan more informative and enjoyable.

ROBBEN W. FLEMING
President
The University of Michigan

The University of Michigan Campus Guide Committee

Kay Cosand
Richard Doolen
Sally Fleming
Kingsbury Marzolf
William Stegath
Robert Warner
Alfred Sussman, *Chairman*

Acknowledgments

Everyone knows that a committee is no way to write a book. Yet, this is exactly the genesis of this *Guide*. The particular qualities of this book are due to this group's conscientious and convivial initiation and development of the process whose conclusion is before us. More than any other element, the committee deserves credit for this book.

The felicitous choice of authors has given substance and form to the committee's ideas. In particular, Margo MacInnes has made what might otherwise have been a catalogue into a graceful and authoritative account of University buildings. Also, my colleagues, E. William Heinrich and Kenneth L. Jones are to be thanked for their authoritative and interesting accounts of the petrology and botany of the campus, respectively.

Publication was greatly expedited by Duane Gifford's staff at University Publications, especially Douglas Hesseltine. The development of the walking tour by Vivian Green helps greatly to enhance the utility of the *Guide*. In addition, the staffs of the offices of Space Analysis and Business Affairs are to be acknowledged for their diligent check of factual information.

Finally, the patient and expert guidance provided the committee by the director of The University of Michigan Press, Walter E. Sears, is gratefully acknowledged, along with the very helpful ministrations of Jean D. Cobb.

ALFRED S. SUSSMAN
Dean of the Graduate School

Contents

Central
Campus

Central Campus

Central Campus

Administration Building

"**Variation** on Mondrian" might be an appropriate title for the distinctive window pattern so integral to the overall design of this building designed by Alden Dow. Opened in 1968, the structure, financed through bonds, made possible a transfer of the University's administrative offices from the LSA Building, now headquarters for the College of Literature, Science, and the Arts.

Dow's six-story building houses the regents room, presidential and vice-presidential offices, and their related units. □

Regents Plaza
Rosenthal Cube

Regents Plaza, extending between the LSA Building and the Administrative Building, was dedicated in June, 1969, in memory of the men and women who had served as regents of the University. It is a favorite spot for occasional rock concerts, frisbee games, and relaxed contemplation of the Cube, a 2,400-pound painted steel sculpture by Michigan alumnus Bernard Rosenthal, that spins on its diagonal axis with a slight push. It is a joint gift of the sculptor and the class of 1965. □

Alumni Memorial Hall
(Museum of Art)

Students disliked the idea. They called it "D'Ooge's Palace" and the "Mausoleum." Professor M. L. D'Ooge was chairman of the committee appointed in 1903 to revive plans for an alumni memorial hall on campus to honor those University men who had died in the Civil War. This was not the first time the subject had come up. In 1864, a committee of the Society of the Alumni of the University was formed to cooperate with the faculty to raise funds for such a memorial.

Not only was it difficult to find financial backing for such a project, but determining just what the function of the building was to be and what was to be housed there was even more complicated. The building was to serve as a meeting place for alumni, and the Department of Fine Arts saw it as the answer to its need for appropriate exhibit and classroom space.

Alumni Memorial Hall, the first building contributed to the University by its alumni, was dedicated May 11, 1910. An appropriate part of the celebration was an exhibition of representative American artists, including a special group of works by Michigan painters, and Oriental and American art from the Charles L. Freer collection.

It was not until the Alumni Association moved into its current location in the Union and Alumni Memorial Hall was substantially altered for the exclusive use of the Museum of Art in 1966–67, that the building was entirely devoted to the arts.

"Nydia" was the first important original work of art acquired for the museum. It was a gift presented to the University in 1862 by alumni and friends from funds raised by citizens of Ann Arbor. The life-size marble is the work of

5

Alumni Memorial Hall
(Museum of Art)

American sculptor Randolph Rogers, who spent his boyhood in Ann Arbor and became one of the leading figures in the later stages of the classical-revival period.

During the ensuing half century, the art collections have continued to grow, most notably with two important bequests. In 1884, Henry C. Lewis bequeathed approximately 600 paintings and other works of art. By the 1950s, Dr. and Mrs. Walter R. Parker of Grosse Pointe, Michigan, had donated their extensive art collection, including art of James Abbott McNeill Whistler, Japanese prints, and the work of midnineteenth-century French artists. The permanent collections now include representative examples of Western and Eastern art from the fifth century to modern times.

A ten-by-thirty-foot steel sculpture titled "Daedalus" is the newest addition. The piece incorporates five parallelograms fanning out to enclose a space almost eleven feet deep. The sculpture was installed on the front lawn of Alumni Memorial Hall in September, 1977, under the direction of its creator Charles Ginnever.

The museum has continued to acquire and display pieces appropriate to its desire to be increasingly responsive to needs of scholars, students, and the University community as a whole.

The museum is open to the public daily from 9:00 to 5:00, Sunday from 1:00 to 5:00; during the summer, daily from 11:00 to 5:00, and Sunday from 1:00 to 5:00. □

James B. Angell Hall

For over a half a century, Angell Hall has been symbol and center of the College of Literature, Science, and the Arts. Completed in 1924, and named for the University's long-tenured president, James Burrill Angell (1871–1909), this monumental office and classroom building is one of several on campus designed by Albert Kahn of Detroit. Erected during the zestful, expansive presidency of Marion L. Burton, Angell Hall was intended, in Burton's words, to "be beautiful, dignified and commanding. It will give unity and form to the entire campus." Burton and the regents felt that a classical design would harmonize with imposing landmarks such as Hill Auditorium, Alumni Memorial Hall, and the President's House. The president's own office was located in Angell Hall until the first Administration Building (now the Literature, Science, and the Arts Building) was finished in 1948.

Sculptor Ulysses Bicci of New York designed the bas relief over the main door, which incorporates symbols traditional to learning and includes the motto on the University's seal: "Artes, Scientia, Veritas." Other icons of wisdom —an owl, a book, the lamp of

learning—appear on panels in the spandrels between the Doric columns. Four larger friezes beside the wide cascade of steps hold anonymous figures comfortably ensconced, depicting "History," "Poetry," and the "Arts," but "Philosophy" bears the likeness of Socrates himself. Carved in stone, high over the facade, is an oft-quoted sentence from the ordinance of 1787 which established the Northwest Territory of which Michigan was a part: "Religion, morality, and knowledge, being necessary to good government and the happiness of mankind, schools and the means of education shall forever be encouraged."

The building has been the victim of campus dissension more than once. One night during the Second World War, but before America's involvement in the conflict, Nazi sympathizers on campus defaced the building's mammoth columns with the painted numbers 1 through 4, daubing a swastika on the fifth column. The heavy-handed symbolism of the incident appeared in a novel with a local setting, *Shadow on the Campus,* written by journalism professor Donald Hamilton Haines.

The lobby ceiling was fashioned by the DiLorenzo Studios of New York, whose artists also decorated the Hatcher Graduate Library and Clements Library. The Hopwood Room, just off the lobby to the south, is a cozy gathering place for campus writers.

Another room down the south corridor has a bronze plaque on its floor designating the spot where, for over fifty years, "stood the class tree of '69, growing to a mighty elm." □

The first separate building for instruction in architecture (and later photography, sculpture, ceramics, landscape architecture, and urban planning) was designed by the University's first dean of architecture, Emil Lorch. Although Lorch planned the structure as an eventual quadrangle, only two wings were built. Instead of completing the original design, the Departments of Art, Architecture and Planning moved into a new building on North Campus in 1974.

For decades before that date, the Old A and D Building was altered, partitioned, and divided to accommodate expanding programs. The library on the second floor was conceded to be the most impressive of the building's inner spaces.

When a program in architectural research was developed, it was necessary to erect a temporary research laboratory in the corner garden. This was the first Unistrut modular building ever assembled, and its construction in 1954 was featured in *Life* magazine. A much older piece of architecture in the garden is the Doric entrance from the Bank of Michigan erected in Detroit in 1836. Professor Emil Lorch rescued it when the building was demolished a century later. Other columns and fragments were acquired to illustrate American architectural styles and classical antecedents. A parade of sassy gargoyles perches atop the low wing of Old A and D's northern wall. □

Burton
Memorial Tower

It has been said that "the first official mention of music made by the University was in reference to bells." A *Michigan Alumnus* writer in 1919 was the first to offer the suggestion that a campanile would be "a practical and beautiful memorial." But it was President Marion L. Burton's enthusiasm that initiated serious consideration to create a centrally located tower with a carillon. It was his untimely death in 1925, however, that provided the real impetus for a fund raising campaign for a carillon dedicated to his memory. In 1935, Charles M. Baird, former University athletic director, provided the funds for the carillon, clock, and tower. The Ann Arbor Alumni Club, the city of Ann Arbor, local friends, and merchants accepted the challenge to provide the additional support.

Work began on the construction of the tower during the 1935–36 school year and Burton Memorial Tower was formally dedicated on December 4, 1936—an appropriate expression of respect to a man whose administration was characterized by unusual financial generosity to the University. Charles Cecil Godfrey, as representative of the bell founders, J. H. Taylor Bell Foundry of

Loughborough, England, and Charles Baird made the formal presentation to President Alexander Ruthven.

The ten-story limestone tower, 212 feet high, now houses the University Musical Society; offices, classrooms, and practice rooms for the School of Music; the studio of the University carillonneur; and on the tenth floor, the sixty-seven bell carillon.

Albert Kahn of Detroit was architect of the unusual plan to construct the building utilizing a reinforced concrete shell faced with limestone rather than solid masonry walls. This plan permitted a larger floor area and a more rigid structure, essential for the support of the 100-ton Baird Carillon, the third heaviest musical instrument in the world.

Largest bell in the carillon, "Big Baird," weighs twelve tons and sounds E-flat below middle C at the stroke of its 350-pound clapper. The smallest bell weighs four pounds and sounds A-sharp, four and one-half octaves higher.

The Baird Carillon is open to the public from April through October on Wednesdays from 4:00 to 5:00 and on Saturdays from 11:00 to 12:00 noon. Recital times and selections are listed in the entrance foyer. Listeners may choose their own comfortable vantage point to hear the bells "call together those who are studious of all good things both human and divine." □

The School of Business Administration was the outgrowth of courses in accounting, finance, marketing, statistics, and business management and organization originally offered within the College of Literature, Science, and the Arts by the Department of Economics. Some of these courses were offered as early as 1900.

Enrollment grew rapidly, particularly during the years immediately following World War I. The School of Business Administration was formally organized in 1924. The present site for the school was authorized by the regents in July, 1945. The building houses thirty classrooms, a laboratory, lecture rooms, student and faculty lounges, and the Business Administration Library.

On December 12, 1973, dedication ceremonies took place for an additional structure, the Assembly Hall, which includes the acoustically perfect, 450-seat Clayton G. Hale Auditorium. Designed by O'Dell, Hewlett and Luckenbach, Assembly Hall offers an attractive lounge area, executive board room with complete kitchen facilities, case discussion rooms, and an executive-in-residence suite for visiting speakers. The building, furnishings, and landscaping were all financed entirely by private gifts.

Newest addition to the Business School quadrangle is the William A. Paton Center for Accounting

School of Business Administration

Education and Research. Opened in 1976, it was funded entirely by private donations from accounting firms, corporations, alumni, and friends of the Business School. The new building allows accounting research and education to be intensified and expanded. Included in the center are the Paton Archives which house materials of the internationally known accountant, economist, author, and teacher for whom the building is named. □

Kalmbach Management Center

Among the many programs offered through the School of Business Administration are workshops and conferences in business management education. The Kalmbach Management Center, located on Washtenaw Avenue, provides continuing education programs for middle-management and executive personnel in private business, industry, and public sector organizations. □

Central Campus Recreation Building and Margaret Bell Pool

There is no doubt that the University is a sports-minded community, both on a personal and a competitive level. A new addition to the recreational facilities is the Central Campus Recreation Building, opened in 1976. The building provides thirteen multipurpose courts used for handball, racquetball, and paddleball, six squash courts, a gymnasium and jogging track, exercise rooms, offices, sauna, and access to Margaret Bell Pool.

Two memorial leaded glass windows, donated by Ruth Hooke of Cincinnati, Ohio, face west from the building. They portray events from both summer and winter Olympics.

Central Campus Recreation Building is open Monday through Friday from 8:00 A.M. to 10:00 P.M.; Saturday from 8:00 to 5:00; Sunday from noon to 10:00. User passes can be purchased by students, faculty, staff, and their families. Alumni and their spouses also can buy a user pass which entitles them to use all of the facilities in the Central Campus Recreation Building, North Campus Recreation Building, Intramural Building, and the Sports Coliseum Building. □

Margaret Bell Pool

As early as 1923, Dr. Margaret Bell, chairperson of the Department of Physical Education for Women, had appealed for a women's swimming pool. It was not until March 10, 1954, however, that the pool became a reality. The modern red brick building was financed by the Board in Control of Intercollegiate Athletics. Many campus organizations, men's and women's, contributed to the Women's Athletic Association Pool Fund used for the furnishing of the pool.

The pool room includes seating for more than 700 people, a six-lane pool, outlets for television cameras and sound equipment, and a window for underwater observation.

A portrait of Dr. Bell, a gift of alumnae of the University, hangs in the lower lobby of the building.

Located behind the Central Campus Recreation Building and Margaret Bell Pool is the Dance Building. It is not part of the recreational facilities. □

Chemistry Building

As early as 1839 chemistry took its place in the curriculum of the University, but initially only as lectures and quizzes. In response to the need for laboratory experience, the first chemical laboratory building at a state university was erected in 1856 at a total cost of about six thousand dollars for building and equipment.

In spite of seven additions made to that structure, natural growth in the numbers of students and in the development of training in dentistry, medicine, engineering, and pharmacy created the need for even larger facilities. By October, 1909, the present building facing the Natural Science Building was sufficiently completed to allow a few courses to christen the laboratories.

The Chemistry Building, designed by Smith, Hinchman and Grylls, originally housed chemistry, pharmacy, and chemical engineering in its crisscrossing corridors and interior courtyards. A major addition in 1948 and new entrances added in 1972 maintain the staid harmony of its buff Indiana limestone and brick exterior.

An amphitheater, classrooms, research rooms, offices, laboratories, and a library serve the rapidly expanding needs of the Department of Chemistry. □

Center for Continuing Education of Women

Tiny office space in the Michigan League Building was the first home for the Center for Continuing Education of Women (CEW). The Center was established in 1964 as a comprehensive service designed to facilitate the reentry of women into higher education and the career marketplace. More than 9,000 men and women have been counseled since then; more than one-half have completed a baccalaureate degree.

Two white frame houses at 328–330 Thompson Street are now the center for CEW services that include counseling, financial assistance information, an exceptional library of vocational and educational reference and loan materials, conferences, small discussion groups, and workshops.

All interested women and men are encouraged to phone, write, or walk in weekdays from 8:30 to 5:00. □

Samuel Trask Dana
Natural Resources
Building

As early as 1903, The University of Michigan offered regular instruction in forestry and conservation. It was the first institution in the United States to do so. Plans for a proposed School of Forestry and Conservation were developed during the spring of 1927 and it opened in September of that year with a faculty of ten and a student body of twenty-five.

The Dana Building, originally West Medical Building, is a Renaissance-style structure faced with dressed fieldstone on the basement and first floor levels. The upper stories are of buff pressed brick with ornamental and molded brick arches and cornices. Two ornamental entrances on the east and west sides of the building are of Bedford limestone. Floors, corridors, and ceilings throughout are of wood; the general finish of the interior is Louisiana red cypress.

Broad program changes were a part of the restructuring that resulted in the establishment of the School of Natural Resources in 1950, providing professional education for practitioners in the fields of forestry, wood technology, wildlife management, and fisheries management. Today, the school includes programs in landscape architecture, recreation policy, administration and design, and environmental education.

In addition to Stinchfield Woods, the school manages Camp Filibert Roth at Golden Lake, Michigan, and maintains a building at the Biological Station at Douglas Lake for teaching and research activity. □

David M. Dennison Physics and Astronomy Building

The 1963 building has offices, lecture rooms, and laboratories for the Department of Physics and Astronomy. The arrangement of one tall and one long, low building joined to form an L solved a serious construction problem in one of the most congested campus areas. □

School of Dentistry Building

Facilities such as those offered in the dental complex could not have been imagined by early faculty and students. The University of Michigan was, in fact, the first state university in the world and the second institution in this country to offer education in dentistry —a profession often considered mere craftsmanship at the time. Practitioners had little technical training and virtually no knowledge of medical or scientific relationships.

The School of Dentistry, established in 1875, had the distinction of having occupied, during its first thirty years of existence, three of the four original professors' houses, the first buildings on the original forty-acre campus. It was an unmistakable sign of things to come.

By 1903, President Angell sought new facilities for the "Dental Department, which [was] wretchedly housed." In October, 1908, the Dental Building, "one of the finest in the entire country," was ready for occupancy,

but by 1923 an addition was needed to accommodate increasing student enrollment and increased curricular requirements.

The first building in the world devoted solely to graduate and postgraduate dental instruction was the W. K. Kellogg Foundation Institute constructed in 1939–40 as an addition to the 1908 building.

Most recent of the School of Dentistry buildings is a four-unit complex adjoining the Kellogg Building.

The Dental Building represents the largest building contract ever made by the University—after more than five years of construction, the complex was completed in 1971 with funds from the W. K. Kellogg Foundation and state and federal sources.

Besides providing space for traditional lecture and laboratory instruction, the building houses a broadcast-quality color television studio and audio-visual and electronic equipment to meet a variety of educational purposes. □

Economics Building

Erected in 1856, the Economics Building is one of the few surviving nineteenth-century edifices on campus. The original portion was a one-story, three-room structure proudly described by President Tappan as "unquestionably . . . unsurpassed by anything of the kind in our country." It was the first chemical laboratory building at any state university, and in fact, the first building in the United States to be designed, erected, and equipped solely for instruction in chemistry.

The section that survives was actually one of the seven additions to the original laboratory built between 1861 and 1901. The Department of Economics moved into the building's south wing in 1909.

A few of the building's historical details remain, including a round window, or "oculus," at the back. The building houses classrooms and department offices. □

Classrooms, auditoriums, media facilities, laboratories, and offices for the School of Education are housed in the former University elementary and secondary laboratory schools. Pleasing use has been made of ceramic tile and marble in the Monroe Street entry. The interior courtyard is particularly pleasant in early May when the trees are in blossom.

The nationally recognized Center for the Study of Higher Education is located in the building, as is the federally funded Educational Resources Information Center and the Education Media Center Library. The first permanent chair devoted exclusively to the training of secondary school teachers and administrators in an American university was established at Michigan in 1879. □

Courses in engineering were first offered at The University of Michigan in 1853. Teasingly dubbed "scientific blacksmiths" by skeptical literary colleagues, Michigan's engineers have ever since been in the vanguard of technological inquiry and innovation.

West Engineering, built in 1904, is the oldest College of Engineering building. Designed by George Mason and Albert Kahn it was known as the New Engineering Building for nearly twenty years, until East Engineering was erected in 1923. A landmark on campus and in the history of engineering education in the United States, West Engineering embodied the latest technical advances of its day. The building's strength is derived from an iron frame, poured concrete floors, and brick and stone walls twelve inches thick. The L-shaped building is embellished with copper-clad cupolas and a broad, red tiled roof.

An enrollment boom resulted in the building of a four-story extension of the north wing, above the naval tank installation. In the 360 foot long tank, the first at any university in this country, tests are run on models large enough to provide accurate data for projecting drag and propeller vibration problems in actual ships. Steel rails along the sides of the tank are traversed by an electric towing device, whose dynamometer measures water resistance at varying speeds. A skimmer clears floating debris from the surface of the tank, while resident goldfish discourage mosquitoes from breeding in the standing water.

The well-known "Engine Arch" which separates the building's north and west wings was the inspiration of Professor Charles Simeon Denison. It was later named the Denison Archway. Above the archway on the building's second level is a student lounge with paneled walls and two ornate fireplaces.

East Engineering Building, designed by the firm of Smith, Hinchman and Grylls, was opened in 1923. Before the North Campus "engineering group" was developed, East Engineering was the principal shop and laboratory. U-shaped, of brick and stone with an ornamental cornice of brick and terracotta, it has a steel frame with reinforced concrete piers for maximum light and space. A south wing was added in 1947 to accommodate growing postwar enrollments. Three structures have been erected on the roof to house laboratories for research in explosives and chemical smokes (1941), illumination (1947), and meteorology (1954).

The College of Engineering has spread to several buldings on the North Campus. See pages 81-84 for information on these buildings. □

The University of Michigan, from its earliest days, has been sensitive to the need for extending its resources state-wide. The first appropriation for such activity was made by the regents in 1912, and since that time, thousands of Michigan residents have taken advantage of courses offered by faculty members through lectures, correspondence, institutes and conferences. The Extension Service operates six regional centers, some of which are part of consortial arrangements with other state institutions. □

Henry S. Frieze Building

Health Service Building

Gentle, shy Henry S. Frieze took over the presidency of the University following the unexpected resignation of Erastus Otis Haven. The building, now named for him, served from 1905 until 1956 as the Ann Arbor High School. The addition of new classroom space in 1957 permits use of the building now by the School of Social Work and several separate departments: Speech Communication and Theater, Linguistics, Near Eastern Studies, Computer and Communication Sciences, and others. □

Dr. Warren E. Forsythe was instrumental in urging the construction of the Health Service Building which was completed in 1940. Architect L. J. Sarvis of Battle Creek designed a building well suited for student health care. Facilities include a pharmacy, infirmary, and clinics. Health services are available to students and their spouses. The facility is open Monday through Friday from 8:00 to 4:30 and on Saturday morning from 8:00 to 11:30. □

Henry S. Frieze Building

Hill Auditorium

The University of Michigan has long been blessed by gifts from alumni, members of its academic community, and friends. In certain periods of its history, private contributions have speeded the construction of needed facilities and radically changed the appearance of the campus. Regent Arthur Hill was one of many individuals who recognized the need and responded generously.

The 4,300-seat auditorium was designed by architects Kahn and Wilby. Paramount among design considerations for its parabolic interior with balcony, gallery, and stage itself capable of seating 300 was the quality of acoustics. Results have been excellent. Experiments and changes made in 1921 and 1949 resulted in an acoustically superior auditorium.

After the installation of a remodeled Frieze Memorial Organ, Hill Auditorium was ready for its dedication on June 25, 1913.

Hill's stated wish that the building be used "for the gathering of students and college body, and their friends," has been met as glee club concerts, orchestras, plays, individual speakers, commencement, and the May Festival have all utilized the building. □

Institute of Human Adjustment, Counseling Division

The Counseling Center building is a handsome specimen of the late nineteenth-century "shingle-style" architecture, a type rare in Ann Arbor. Built in 1891, it was originally the residence of University Regent Charles Adolphus Whitman.

Shingle dwellings of the 1880s and 90s sparked a reaction against the stiff formality of Victorian houses whose rooms were elegant, isolated boxes. Here the central "living hall" with its grand fireplace, inglenooks, and staircase became the comfortable, symbolic heart of the home, foreshadowing the open interiors of the next century's functional architecture. Exposed beams made the ceiling appear lower, creating more intimate space.

The building's foundation and lower story assembled from native fieldstones support two upper floors whose outer walls are decorated with California redwood shingles. Local newspapers boasted that the house had been finished in "the best woods obtainable." Major rooms have wainscoting, and the staircase is of golden oak. Doors offer medieval-looking hand-wrought hardware for the visitor's grasp.

A gazebo at the back once provided a view across the Huron River's hills, but later buildings have blocked that splendid scene. Mr. Whitman's carriage barn has vanished also, but the porte-cochere remains across the driveway, a visible reminder of Ann Arbor's horse-and-buggy days. □

Kelsey Museum of Archaeology (Newberry Hall)

The Kelsey Museum of Archaeology houses one of the nation's finest collections of artifacts from ancient Greece, Italy, North Africa, and the Near East. It is an appropriate memorial to Francis W. Kelsey, professor of Latin language and literature at the University from 1889 to 1927. It was he who added a museum course in archaeology and seminars in the study of Roman coins and lamps, foreshadowing an enthusiasm that culminated, in 1924, in the University's first field work in archaeology in the Near East.

Gifts from faculty, students, and citizens of Detroit and Ann Arbor, including one gift from Mrs. Helen H. Newberry of Detroit, provided the funds necessary for construction of Newberry Hall, named in honor of her husband Judge John S. Newberry (1847).

While actual plans were prepared by Rohn and Spier of Detroit, the 1891 building stands as an excellent example of the kind of work for which architect H. H. Richardson of Boston became famous.

Native fieldstone from the surrounding countryside sealed with

Kelsey Museum of Archaeology (Newberry Hall)

grout and mortar forms the structure and facade over the windows and doorways. The circular tower —a Richardson trademark— encloses the stairway to the balcony that once overlooked a second floor auditorium. An unusual checkerboard pattern and a cross in the exterior stonework combine with wood paneling and decorative glass inside to enhance the charm of one of the University's oldest buildings.

A gradual transition in the use of the building proceeded from its use in 1904 as a center for the Young Women's Christian Association through a period as classrooms and lecture hall for University classes. Structural changes in 1928 adapted it for use as a museum for the Department of Classical Studies. By 1937 the board of directors of the old Students Christian Association had transferred the property to the University for $1.00.

Today, enriched by exceptional acquisitions, the museum is known particularly for its textiles, chiefly Roman, Coptic, and Islamic. The interior of the building has undergone extensive revision and adaptation to better serve the needs of staff, students, and the general public. Special exhibits and lectures are offered in the spirit of Francis Kelsey's dedication to the "effective fostering of scholarly ideals."

The museum is open to the public from mid-September to June 1 on Monday through Friday from 9:00 to 4:00; Saturday and Sunday from 1:00 to 4:00. The summer schedule (June to mid-September) is Monday through Friday from 11:00 to 4:00; Saturday and Sunday from 1:00 to 4:00. □

Edward Henry Kraus Natural Science Building

Lane Hall

The Edward Henry Kraus Natural Science Building was a "gift" of the state legislature in response to a 1913 request, during the presidency of Harry Burns Hutchins, for facilities to relieve cramped classrooms and lack of laboratory space. With the appropriation, construction began in October, 1913, based on plans by architect Albert Kahn of Detroit.

Externally, the building resembles its neighbor Hill Auditorium—dark tapestry brick with light stone and terra-cotta trim. On the interior, however, Kahn utilized a newly developed system of construction using regularly spaced steel and concrete piers to provide structural support, leaving the space between piers available for flexible room arrangement and maximum utilization of window areas. Designed to house the Departments of Botany, Forestry, Geology, Mineralogy, Psychology, and Zoology, each discipline was assigned a vertical section from basement to roof, permitting the installation of heavy machinery for special apparatus and excellent facilities for shipping, receiving, and storage materials. Space for the Division of Biology and winter quarters for Biological Station personnel are the perfect functions of the building. Common areas are used for lecture rooms, offices, display space, and laboratories, A small pond in the center courtyard is known as Lake Woodhead in honor of former professor Arthur E. Woodhead.

In 1973 the building was renamed the Edward Henry Kraus Building in honor of the former dean of the College of Pharmacy, dean of the College of Literature, Science, and the Arts, and distinguished mineralogist. □

Since 1963, five Asian Studies Centers have been housed in the building concurrently, prompting its use as the nerve center for arrangements for the 1967 International Congress of Orientalists. As such, it is particularly remembered by hundreds of scholars from Europe, Asia, and North Africa. In a sense, Lane Hall carries on one of its early legacies—to work with foreign students on the Michigan campus.

Acquired by the University in 1937 and named in honor of Judge Victor H. Lane, a member of the Law School faculty and long time president of the YMCA, it is an excellent example of the Georgian-style architecture on campus, notable for its large-paned windows, double French doors, mansard roof, and dormers.

Of particular interest is the interior lobby of Lane Hall, converted in 1970 to a Japanese-style garden with lounging platforms and landscaped pool. The building is open to interested visitors Monday through Friday from 8:00 to 5:00. □

Law Quadrangle

The magnificent buildings comprising the Law Quadrangle were given to the University by alumnus William W. Cook (1880, 1882L) who amassed a fortune during his career as general counsel for the Commercial Cable and Postal Telegraph Company. Cook, who had already donated funds for construction of the Martha Cook Building, wished "to aid in enlarging the scope and improving the standards of the law schools" through additional benefactions to the Law School at The University of Michigan.

In addition to an endowment for legal research, Cook's plan called for construction of two dormitories, a library, and an office and classroom building. Two city blocks, formerly bisected by Haven Street, were occupied by the new buildings and the broad, elm-shaped lawn which they enclosed. Erected during the decade 1923–33, the structures exhibit a harmony of architectural style. In its reliance on dignified, traditional styles, the Law Quadrangle is an appropriate setting for a scholarly discipline founded upon centuries of precedent.

Law Quadrangle

The buildings recall the Tudor-Gothic style of the colleges of Oxford and Cambridge and the Inns of Court in London. The architects, York and Sawyer of New York, also claimed Scottish models for their work. The Lawyers Club tower resembles the entrance to the Clock Court in Hampton Court Palace, and the dining hall is obviously a condensed version of Kings College Chapel in Cambridge. The group as a whole is constructed of Weymouth seam-faced granite, trimmed in Indiana limestone. □

William W. Cook Legal Research Building

Opened in 1931, and named by the University's regents for its donor, who had died a year earlier, this is the most striking building of the quadrangle group—bold, rugged and massive. Its chief attraction is the vast library reading room, with seating for 450 scholars. No other room on campus approaches this awesome space in decorative splendor, from the paneled and medallioned plaster ceiling to the floor of quiet cork.

Under the ceiling's heavy tie-beams, fierce creatures—lions rampant, hawks and griffins—leer down at oblivious readers far below. The stone walls are paneled in carved oak to a height of fifteen feet, above which high windows of tinted glass filter soft light into the room. Stained-glass windows bear seals of the colleges and universities of the world. Ten thousand volumes line the walls of this room, and another twenty thousand are tucked into long, narrow alcoves which flank the building on both sides.

Thirty-two offices fill the floor above the reading room. William W. Cook's own library is also there—an exact duplicate of the room in his New York home—filled with his own books, furniture, and mementos.

The Law Library, which now houses 450,000 volumes, is rapidly filling up. An addition will soon become necessary, but an astronomical rise in the cost of stone construction since the 1930s precludes any attempt to match the existing quadrangle structures.

Architect Gunnar Birkerts seems to have found a solution to the problem of blending necessarily modern structures with existing Gothic architecture. The newest library addition will be an underground facility with a 150-foot-long skylight that will project daylight into the subterranean building and will also give users an unobstructed view of the surrounding buildings. The structure is expected to be completed by spring, 1980. □

John P. Cook Residence Hall

This additional dormitory was planned as a memorial to the donor's father. The building, opened in the fall of 1930, is one story higher than the Lawyers Club, its rooms somewhat larger, its appointments slightly better. The memorial room, with carved, paneled oak walls and stained glass windows, contains a full-length portrait of John Poller Cook, painted by Henry Caro-Delvaille. Diligent connoisseurs of detail will discover at least seventy-six impudent faces beside many of the building's windows and doors. □

Law Quadrangle

Hutchins Hall

Hutchins Hall was the last of the quadrangle buildings, a classroom and office structure which opened in 1933. It was named, at Mr. Cook's request, for the late Harry B. Hutchins, who had been dean of the Law School from 1895 to 1910 and president of the University from 1910 to 1920. Hutchins was the first alumnus and the first faculty member to ascend to that office. Inside the building, first floor corridor windows overlook a small garden court. Window panes contain whimsical etchings on tinted glass, each drawing satirizing a different specimen of legal terminology.

An alumni room on the first floor contains pictures of all law classes since 1873. On the second floor is the practice courtroom, an innovation pioneered at Michigan by the late Professor Edson R. Sunderland. □

Lawyers Club

Renaissance influences are visible in the "cloister" of Doric columns at the northwest corner of the quadrangle, as well as in the Lawyers Club Lounge itself. The floor is of wide white oak, fastened with dowels. Dark oak paneling, a fireplace, a huge bay window, and tapestries enhance the attractiveness of this room, which is the social center for residents of the quadrangle. The marble-floored dining hall is another splendid room. Its ceiling, fifty feet high, is sustained by beams carved from old ship timbers. Busts of famous barristers and jurists, among them Solon, Justinian, Grotius, Blackstone, Coke, Story, Webster, Marshall, and Michigan's own Thomas M. Cooley, decorate the beams.

Opened in 1924, the Lawyers Club was the first of the quadrangle buildings to be completed. Its dormitory wing extends two blocks eastward from the lounge corner, along South University Avenue. Each of its nine units has a separate entrance. In an archway under the tower are six fascinating gargoyles, small figures wearing faces of the presidents who served the University until 1925. Henry P. Tappan, Michigan's first president (1852–63), and James B. Angell, who had the longest tenure (1871–1909), recline above the doors, Tappan on the east wall, Angell on the west. In the corner south of the Tappan figure is one of his successors, E. O. Haven (1863–69), and to the north, a figure of Henry S. Frieze, three times acting president (1869–71, 1881, 1887). North of the Angell piece is a sculpture of his successor, Harry B. Hutchins (1910–20), former dean of the Law School, for whom Hutchins Hall was later named. The south figure on the west wall represents Marion LeRoy Burton (1920–25), who died in office the year after this building was finished. Sixteen other figures, playfully depicting scholars, athletes, and members of various professions, decorate the quadrangle's east and west archway entrances.

Sumptuous in scale and lavish in ornament, the quadrangle buildings contain many pleasant rewards for the visitor. □

Libraries

The entire library system of The University of Michigan includes twenty-one divisional libraries, seven departmental and area collections, four special libraries, the Harlan Hatcher Graduate Library and the Undergraduate Library. Total University volumes number close to five million.

Center for Afroamerican and African Studies Library

Since 1971 the Center for Afroamerican and African Studies has offered dual programs of instruction and research leading toward service to the larger community as its central goal. The CAAS library on Haven Street provides audio-visual and printed materials for faculty and student use. Kuumba murals on the exterior of the library are the work of students. ☐

William L. Clements Library of Americana

The collection of 47,000 books, 300,000 manuscripts, letters, and documents, 4,200 volumes of newspapers and 36,000 maps of American history from Columbus to the end of the Civil War ranks as one of the finest in the United States. This is the priceless treasure preserved in the William L. Clements Library.

Regent William L. Clements enjoyed a casual interest in early American literature that became a passion culminating in a gift to the University of his extensive collection and a magnificent building in which to house it. Clements devoted himself primarily to original source materials printed prior to 1800.

The building, one of many planned for the campus by Albert Kahn of Detroit, was designed

William L. Clements Library of Americana

---

under the careful direction of Clements himself, who specified the Italian Renaissance style. Executed in Indiana limestone, the terraced entrance leads to three rounded archways ornamented with vaulted ceilings of blue and gold mosaic. Carvings above the bronze entrance doors depict the arms of Columbus, The University of Michigan, and the House of Stuart.

Legends carved on the facade, "In darkness dwells the people which knows its annals not," and "Tradition fades but the written record remains ever fresh," are not classical quotations as one might expect, but rather compositions of Professor Ulrich B. Phillips, noted historian on the University faculty in 1923.

The hushed interior main room is lined with bookcases below oak paneling two stories high. Exhibit cases prominently display materials taken from the storage areas that guard them against fire, theft, and atmospheric damage.

In his meticulous fashion, Clements set forth what he conceived to be the duties of the University in maintaining the building and in providing proper staff. At the June, 1923, dedication ceremony, he spoke of his gift as "primarily a library for advanced research on the part of scholars already well equipped, rather than a library . . . for either the undergraduate or the ordinary graduate student." Regent Clements chose the first director himself, Randolph Greenfield Adams, who early recognized the necessity to "mediate between being hospitable and being careful." Cautious stewardship of his fragile charge annoyed students and faculty accustomed to easy access to library materials. In defense, Adams published a brochure in 1925, explaining *The Whys and Wherefores of the William L. Clements Library.* Access to the collections is still restricted to serious scholars of early American history, and readers are interviewed by the director. All of the important historians of the American Revolution in the past fifty years have used the library at one time or another, including Samuel Eliot Morison, Bruce Catton, Allen Nevins, and Carl Van Doren.

The exhibit room is open to the public Monday through Friday from 9:00 to 12:00 and from 1:00 to 5:00. □

Libraries

Harlan Hatcher Graduate Library

How would you approach the task of establishing the core collection for a university library? Reverend John Monteith, first president of the University of Michigania, apparently found it quite simple. His diary entry for May 5, 1816, reads: "Purchase the library and do some other business."

It was Asa Gray, one of the most famous American botanists of the century, who was charged by the regents in 1838 to purchase a library in Europe with the appropriated $5,000 plus $1,500 for his expenses. This designation of funds by the regents is indica-

tive of early interest and concern for the availability of a library on campus. Even more impressive is the purchase that same year of one of 200 copies of Audubon's *Birds of America*. At $950, it was a staggering expenditure for a fledgling institution. The book remains one of the library's most treasured possessions.

By 1847, the regents were making regular appropriations for the library, a mostly wooden structure destroyed in 1895 as a serious fire hazard.

The new library was dedicated at ceremonies held in Hill Auditorium on January 7, 1920. The building stands on the site of the old building, enveloping the original bookstacks, virtually the only

Libraries

fireproof section of the original building. It was, for its time, a miracle of economy and efficiency. Still, there was room for "luxuries" such as the vaulted main reading room and broad marble staircases. Frescoes by Gari Melchers, "The Arts of War" and "The Arts of Peace," painted in 1893 for the Manufacturers' Building at the Chicago World's Fair, decorate the lunettes above the windows at either end of the reading room.

There is, however, a sort of Parkinson's Law that applies to libraries: any improvement in facilities stimulates the demand placed on them. Before long, the light wells were floored in, stack levels raised and, in 1970, an addition was opened. Along with this expansion, divisional and special libraries were growing, as well as special collections.

One particularly noteworthy example is the Department of Rare Books and Special Collections. Original documents, manuscripts, eyewitness accounts, and first editions are all available for scholarly research. The manuscript collection includes an extraordinary group of Greek New Testament manuscripts and Islamic writings. The papyrus collection, foremost of its kind in this country, includes papyri dating from the third century B.C. to the eighth century A.D. The nationally known Labadie collection of materials on political and social protest and economic and labor history is used by faculty and graduate students across the country.

The library is open Monday through Thursday, from 8:00 A.M. to midnight; Friday from 8:00 A.M. to 10:00 P.M.; Saturday from 10:00 A.M. to 6:00 P.M.; and Sunday from 1:00 P.M. to midnight. □

Libraries

Undergraduate Library

In 1954, partially to relieve pressure on the Graduate Library facilities, the University library staff and an advisory committee of architectural and administrative members considered plans for an undergraduate library.

Students' disrespectful nickname for it, the "UGLI," does not inhibit their use of the building. It is one of the most used resources on campus by both graduate and undergraduate students. In 1976–77 total building attendance topped 1,250,000.

Its popularity is not surprising. It was the second in the nation to be built as a separate facility for undergraduates, and has been recognized as "one of the most efficient purveyors of reading matter in the world both in design and in procedures." The building was dedicated February 21, 1958, after more than four years of intensive planning that culminated in a library not only extraordinarily responsive to Michigan students' needs, but one with many unique features.

Exhibit areas and a print study gallery make works of art readily available. With services such as eight outside book return chutes —an innovation at the time— unusually large audio-visual facilities, a lounge, soundproofed reading rooms for the blind, and a small movie theater for multimedia lectures, the structure earns its accolades.

Selection of the approximately 50,000 books available at the opening of the new facility required only three years to complete. The goal was to satisfy the undergraduate's normal library needs—whether for assigned, recommended, or independent reading—through four years of study in any discipline from accounting to zoology.

Today, students have available to them more than 180,000 volumes. The plan by architect Albert Kahn still functions well in providing "the most usable collection in the most workable environment." More than being workable, the library is a congenial and pleasant place to study. □

College of Literature, Science, and the Arts Building

Quickly dubbed the "salmon loaf" because of the peculiar orange tint of its brick exterior, the Literature, Science, and the Arts (LSA) Building was the Administration Building for the first twenty-three years of its existence.

Beside the main entrance are two bronze sculptures by Michigan's Marshall Fredericks, who also erected the gigantic figure of the "Spirit of Detroit" at the foot of Woodward Avenue in the Motor City. His "Dream of the Young Man" evokes the quest of adventure, but the implied domestic yearning of "Dream of the Young Girl" has drawn critical fire in recent years.

When the new Administration Building was completed in 1968, several LSA departments moved into the "salmon loaf," and the name was changed to reflect the new occupants. The building is the headquarters for the largest of the University's eighteen schools and colleges. In addition to the administrative offices, the registrar, cashier, and several other all-University offices occupy the first two floors. The University's FM radio station, WUOM, remains on the top floor. □

Clarence C. Little Science Building

Mason and Haven Halls

Formerly the East Medical Building, this red brick structure with white stone trim is recognizably an Albert Kahn building. Ground was broken late in October, 1923, following a visit in March of that year by the entire state legislature, which came to Ann Arbor to survey the campus and listen to a plea for funds from President Marion Burton.

The building, opened in 1925, is now connected to the College of Pharmacy Building and provides facilities for both pharmacy and natural sciences students and faculty. □

These utilitarian structures, completed in 1952, answered a pressing need for classroom and office space. Linked to Angell Hall by a new wing of four auditoriums, Haven and Mason replaced University Hall, formerly the main building of the campus, and old Haven Hall, the original (1863) Law Building, which was destroyed by fire in 1950.

Classrooms and offices are physically separated in the Mason-Haven complex. Mason Hall, the classroom wing, perpetuates the name of the University's first classroom structure which had honored Michigan Governor Stevens T. Mason, the first president (ex-officio) of the Board of Regents. In 1912 the Daughters of the American Revolution put a plaque on the original building bearing the inscription "Mason Hall/1842"—a year later than the actual date of construction. The error persists; the marker was saved and now decorates the north entrance of the "new" Mason Hall.

Haven Hall, hailed as the first skyscraper on campus, contains 188 offices. On the ground floor, near the elevators, hangs the original Haven Hall framed directory board salvaged after the fire in 1950. The lobby connecting Mason and Haven Halls was immediately dubbed the "fishbowl" by students amazed to see an entire wall of glass. Today glass walls are commonplace, but the name lingers. □

Michigan League

"Co-Eds at Ann Arbor Shine Shoes to Get Funds for Clubhouse," the headline read. This article which appeared in a 1923 issue of the weekly *Detroit Saturday Night* noted that one gentleman even had his tan shoes blacked by an overenthusiastic young lady. Under the fund-raising motto "She Stoops to Conquer," women students and alumnae polished shoes and undertook a variety of novel money-making schemes to raise funds for construction of the Michigan League.

Their goal was to provide a building that was to be unique in the history of American state universities—a spacious, well-appointed setting for social, recreational, and residential needs of the women at The University of Michigan. It was to be in all respects a counterpart to the successful Michigan Union then open only to male students. In February, 1921, the initial planning for the building was begun under President Marion LeRoy Burton. The need for such facilities was later acknowledged by the regents with these words: "Facilities for . . . women students and for the housing of their extracurricular activities . . . have been in late years utterly inadequate, if not wholly non-existent." The regents agreed to furnish the site if alumnae could raise the funds to construct and endow the building.

The challenge was accepted, and gifts came in from around the world. The first large gift was donated by Robert Lamont (1896) of Chicago, for the establishment of a memorial to the League's first president, Mrs. Ethel Hussey.

A gift from Gordon Mendelssohn provided the beautiful 700-seat Lydia Mendelssohn Theater as a memorial to his mother. Chinese alumnae in Tientsin sent antique tapestries made from a royal Manchu dynasty robe. Oriental rugs, vases, silver pieces, pianos, and other furnishings were donated by alumnae across the country.

"The dream of Michigan women for 38 years assumed the more concrete form of stone when on Thursday, March 29 [1928], the cornerstone of the new Women's League Building was laid." Formal dedication ceremonies were held June 14, 1929, to celebrate a feat labeled as "the most significant event in the history of the Michigan coed."

Architects Pond and Pond, the same firm that had designed the Michigan Union, created a building of serenity, grace, and utility with meeting rooms, dining rooms, a theater, a library, a ballroom, hotel accommodations, and a garden court, where men were not allowed without an escort.

Visitors are delighted with the strong architectural motif softened with red brick and white stone trim and balanced with graceful dormers, alcoves, and balconies.

Handcrafted tile floors and stained glass windows enhance the atmosphere of congeniality and purpose.

Today, the League has a more coeducational focus as joint Union/League activities have developed and the availability of apartments, dormitories, fraternities, and sororities meet student needs.

Lydia Mendelssohn Theater, christened in the spring of 1929, creates much of the League activity with resident and professional companies offering performances almost year round. Basil Rathbone, Grace Kelly, Jimmy Stewart, and Helen Hayes are but a few of the players who have performed there and stayed as guests at the League. Students, staff, and alumni still use the meeting rooms, cafeterias, and the elegantly appointed dining rooms on the second floor.

On the mall in front of the League's main entrance is a fountain designed by Swedish sculptor Carl Milles. It represents Triton, Greek god of the sea, frolicking in the waves with his piscine children. The fountain, a gift of Charles Baird, who also donated Burton Tower, is named in honor of his friend Thomas M. Cooley, professor of law. ☐

Michigan Union

Some have called it "the best embodiment of Michigan spirit." Certainly the Michigan Union building, a model for student unions at major colleges and universities around the country, has been the center of some of the happiest moments on the Ann Arbor campus.

The present building is a successor to an earlier Union Club House. Early in 1916, in response to a need for expanded facilities, the Union Club House was torn down to make room for the present Union, designed by the brothers Irving K. and Allen B. Pond of Chicago on a scale unheard of at that time.

Early fund raising capitalized on widespread interest and enthusiasm of students and alumni. Union dues, popular Michigan Union Opera, and the adoption of a Union button worn by all student members laid the groundwork for pride in the organization. But the building was not destined to a speedy and uncomplicated completion.

Actual construction began in 1916 as President Harry B. Hutchins turned the first shovelful of sod during commencement. Preliminary building plans had involved only the construction of the shell of the building, with interior finishing and furnishing to

Michigan Union

be completed as additional funds were received, an arrangement seriously stalled by America's entry into the war. The shell was crudely converted to barracks and mess hall for use by 3,600 members of the Students Army Training Corps for the duration of the war.

By the time of its official opening in the fall of 1919, the building and the concept of the Union had assumed a warmly acknowledged role in University life—it was "a hearthstone away from home." Wood paneled wainscoting and terra-cotta tile floors accent the grace and warmth of wide corridors and comfortable lounges. Carved in the stonework bracketing the main entrance are two figures representing an athlete and a scholar. The academic community once reveled in dinners and dancing to ten-piece orchestras in the elegant ballroom. Meeting rooms, a swimming pool, and the Pendleton Library served faculty, students, and alumni, who enjoyed the use of forty-nine guest rooms, a barber shop, and dining rooms.

That is to say, the men of the University enjoyed them since the Union was designated from its inception as a refuge for male members. One concession permitted the designation of a ladies dining room (since women were not even permitted as guests in the regular dining rooms) near the north side entrance to the building, firmly established as the "ladies' entrance" and strictly enforced by the doorkeeper. It was

not until 1954 that women were formally permitted front door access to the Union.

To the left of the entrance, mounted on the stone facade, is a plaque commemorating the first public announcement of the Peace Corps made by John F. Kennedy on October 14, 1960, while he was campaigning in Ann Arbor. A brass marker on the second step identifies the exact spot on which he stood while addressing the students.

Today, among the Union's many facilities are guest rooms, student organization offices, a fast-food concession, a bookstore, an art gallery (open Tuesday–Saturday, 10:00 to 5:00), alumni offices, barbershop, bowling alley, and billiard room. □

International Center

Michigan has had a special interest in foreign students ever since President James B. Angell went to China as minister plenipotentiary in 1880-81. In his enthusiastic endorsement of international relations, President Clarence C. Little once entertained a group of foreign students at his home with an old-fashioned lumberjack supper at which he required his startled guests to eat their meal—including baked beans—with only a knife.

Today the International Center is housed in the Michigan Union. Its goals are more broadly represented now as it seeks to provide programs and information for both foreign and American students. Immigration, employment, health, and travel questions are but a few of the mutual areas of interest.

The center works closely with the Ann Arbor community and the English Language Institute to meet the needs of foreign students and visitors. □

Michigan Alumni Association

As of September, 1977, approximately 240,688 individuals are degree holders of The University of Michigan. The Alumni Association, currently housed on the lower level of the Union, provides active programs and benefits for its membership, such as the activities of over 140 alumni clubs throughout the world, an opportunity to enjoy overseas tours and family camps. Membership in the association includes a subscription to *Michigan Alumnus,* the second oldest existing alumni publication in the country and the first alumni monthly. In fact, immediately after commencement exercises on the day the first University of Michigan class was graduated, August 6, 1845, novice alumni met to form a Society of Alumni. The mutual enrichment derived from this association throughout the years is almost inestimable. □

The University Club

It started as an organization to encourage fencing and boxing among faculty members. The time was December, 1911, and its primary instigator was Professor Carl Leonard DeMuralt. The club abandoned early plans for its own building and prospered in the basement of Alumni Memorial Hall, although the refusal of the regents to provide showers discouraged the sporting members.

By 1938 the new south wing of the Michigan Union provided new quarters with a lounge, pool table, a library, and food service for club members.

The University Club is now thought of primarily as the terrace and dining room facility at the west end of the main floor concourse of the Union. Memberships in the University Club are available to faculty, staff, students and their parents, spouses and members of their immediate family, alumni and emeriti, and individuals retired from University positions. □

Modern Language Building

This four-story classroom and office building designed by Albert Kahn was winner of the 1972 Honors Award of the Detroit Chapter of the American Institute of Architects. Its long, layered facade encloses offices, language laboratories, and classrooms for instruction in modern languages. The two large auditoriums are often used for the showing of noncommercial film series and for guest lectures. □

Neuroscience Laboratory Building

North Hall

The Neuroscience Laboratory Building, formerly the Food Service Building, was built in 1948 and was remodeled in 1970-71 to house various research laboratories. This facility, located midway between the School of Medicine and the Central Campus, is part of an interdisciplinary and interdepartmental effort by the University to facilitate research and teaching in the neurosciences.

The first floor of the building presently houses the research activities of scientists affiliated with the Mental Health Research Institute, Department of Psychiatry. The second floor houses the research activities of scientists affiliated with the Department of Psychology, including ophthalmology, electrical and computer engineering, and biology. Renovation of the ground floor is presently underway and will house the research activities of scientists affiliated with the Departments of Neurology and Anesthesiology. The building also houses the laboratories for the neuroscience doctoral program. □

At its formal opening in December, 1900, the Homeopathic Medical College building, now known as North Hall, was said to afford "ample clinical facilities for years to come." In subsequent years the building housed the University Extension Service, army, air force, and naval ROTC units, the American Red Cross, and the Audio-Visual Education Center. Currently, it once again serves ROTC units on campus. □

North University Building

In 1914 the Department of Buildings and Grounds served as architect and contractor for the construction of a storehouse and shop building to provide offices for the superintendent, maintenance and construction materials, and space for janitor and hospital supplies. Railroad tracks fed into the building, and it is said that at one time part of the building was used as a stable for the horses that pulled snowplows.

It is known now as the North University Building and houses two major academic units and several smaller ones. The University Herbarium, a collection of more than 1½ million scientific specimens of plants from around the world, is distinguished as being one of few herbaria in the United States chosen to be supported as a regional rather than a state or national facility. It is supported by grants from the National Science Foundation and provides research facilities for faculty, graduate students, and through special arrangements, to researchers from other institutions. The herbarium is not open to the general public, although staff members will identify plants for anyone who requests it.

The herbarium shares this building with the English Language Institute. Begun in 1941, the institute provides English language instruction for foreign students, trains teachers to teach English as a second language, does research, and develops texts and teaching materials which are sold all over the world. □

Observatory

The University Observatory was built in 1854 with funds donated largely by citizens of Detroit. For that reason, it was originally called the Detroit Observatory. The confusing name was changed in 1931. An unusual structure for a small frontier college such as Ann Arbor had then, the building helped fulfill Henry Philip Tappan's dream of Michigan becoming a true university—literally embracing the universe.

Isolated on a hilltop in what was then open countryside, Tappan's building combined the symmetry of classical-revival architecture—expressed in the Doric portico and balanced wings—with the typical cube shape and bracketed eaves of the popular Italian style then sweeping the Midwest. The stucco outer walls were scored in a pattern of large blocks to resemble masonry, a pretentious but economical embellishment also used on the University's eight previous buildings.

The Observatory was capped by a rotating dome twenty-one feet in diameter.

Inside the building one may see the first large telescope ever constructed in the United States, a twelve-inch refractor which has been in continuous use for over 120 years. When it was installed in 1854, it was the third largest lens in the world. The telescope is supported on a tapering pier of solid masonry which extends fifteen feet below the surface and floats on a pad in a volume of sand, resting free of the walls to protect it from jarring vibrations from the nearby railroad.

The meridian circle in the east wing is a smaller telescope, which does not rotate. It was used originally to compute time from observations of stars "crossing" the longitudinal (north-south) meridian.

An astronomer using the meridian circle worked in an awkward position because the instrument

had to be pointed directly upward at the heavens. A padded bench beneath it helped to mitigate discomfort. This observation couch was adjustable, rolling on a short track in the floor. It, too, has survived the years, as have several accessory instruments.

The Department of Astronomy today has more sophisticated telescopes, and is housed in newer buildings, but it has not forsaken the hill where it began. One of the state's oldest landmark structures, the Observatory was recently entered in the National Register of Historic Places. ☐

"**Whereas** the University of Michigan College of Pharmacy, founded in 1876, was the first in the nation to offer a full-time university program in pharmacy. . . ." Thus Michigan State Senate resolution number 551 recently saluted the one-hundredth anniversary of the College of Pharmacy.

The building currently housing the College of Pharmacy is but the most recent in a number of structures that have housed pharmacy students and faculty. The original Chemistry-Pharmacy Building, built in 1856, featured the first chemistry laboratory in a state university. Nine years later, degrees were granted in pharmaceutical chemistry to twenty-three students, the first of such degrees in the nation.

In 1960, the College of Pharmacy's new location was completed. It was paid for by a grant from the U.S. Public Health Service, gifts from alumni, University sources, the pharmaceutical industry, and friends of the college. It is joined to the C. C. Little Science Building to provide facilities within the two buildings for administrative offices, counseling, laboratories, research in specialized areas, and the Walgreen Pharmaceutical Center with its modern professional practice laboratory, audio-visual center, and service facilities.

Meticulous and energetic Albert B. Prescott, appointed as first dean of the College of Pharmacy in 1876, would be proud of the exceptional graduates of his college which include Josiah K. Lilly, John G. Searle, Charles R. Walgreen, Jr., Charles R. Walgreen III, and the twins, Amelia and Mary Upjohn, daughters of the founder of the Upjohn Pharmaceutical Company. ☐

Power Center for the Performing Arts

It reflects both literally and figuratively. The mirrored facade of the Power Center for the Performing Arts is set at the edge of Felch Park. At night, when the interior lobby is lit, the gathering theater audience is clearly visible through the special glass facade. Inside, two free-standing spiral staircases arc over the lobby walls, highlighted by two tapestries, Picasso's "Volutes" and Lichtenstein's "Modern Tapestry." The building is known for its architectural beauty and its flexible stage design executed by architects Kevin Roche-John Dinkeloo and Associates of Hamden, Connecticut.

An unusual stage arrangement allows the orchestra pit to convert the more conventional proscenium stage into a thrust stage, projecting sixteen feet into the auditorium. In order to maintain the intimacy of a small theater, the 1,420 seats are arranged in a semicircular shape with no seat farther away from the stage than seventy-two feet.

A movable stage lift for the orchestra platform can stop at four levels—stage, house, orchestra, and pit. The stage tower rises ninety-three feet above the stage to allow for raising and lowering scenery and curtains.

The Power Center is named in honor of the family of Eugene B. Power, former U-M regent, who contributed a major portion of the funding for its construction, making possible a broad range of student and professional dance, instrumental, and dramatic productions. Additional gifts have been made by alumni and friends of the University—a reflection of the long outstanding interest in and generous support for the arts at The University of Michigan. □

President's House

Of the University's nine presidents, all but one have lived in this house, which has been altered and enlarged several times since its construction in 1840. One of the original campus buildings, and now the oldest to survive, it was one of four identical faculty residences built along dignified classical-revival lines. All were of brick covered with smooth stucco scored to resemble large blocks of stone. Used also in construction of the first classroom buildings, and promptly imitated by builders in the town, this deceptive stucco technique soon earned Ann Arbor a distinctive nickname, "the little stucco village."

The University had no chief executive until 1852 when Henry Philip Tappan commenced his brisk and imperious reign. Tappan piped gaslight into the house, but made no other changes. The house as he knew it had a simple, formal plan: two stories, each with four rooms, two on each side of a central hallway. Each room had a fireplace—the only source of heat.

During the time Erastus Otis Haven, Tappan's amiable successor, lived in the house, a small kitchen wing was added. An abstemious Methodist clergyman, he was dismayed to discover a huge basement accumulation of empty wine bottles left behind by the Presbyterian Tappan, who, though himself a man of the cloth, had entertained his dinner guests with cosmopolitan flair.

The President's House was the first in Ann Arbor to be equipped with indoor plumbing and a flush toilet, installed as a condition of James B. Angell's coming in 1871. Angell literally raised the roof during his long tenure, adding a third story which reshaped the house in the fashionable Italianate mode, with brackets supporting an overhanging cornice. A New England "widow's walk" capped the low-pitched roof. In 1891 a west wing was

added, giving Angell a semicircular library. Partitions were removed and rooms enlarged. Electricity was introduced.

Harry Burns Hutchins, dean of the Law School, already had a house near campus when he was appointed to succeed Angell, who retired in 1909 after thirty-eight years in office. Angell was thus able to live out his days in the house.

Unoccupied after Angell's death in 1916, the house became a Red Cross station during World War I.

Despite his untimely death in 1925, five years after he moved in, Marion LeRoy Burton left his mark on the President's House. His tenure marked an ambitious building program on campus. Burton transformed his residence as well, adding a simple porch on the east side with a porch above it, enclosing the back porch for dining, and placing a garage with overhead bedroom at the back. Burton's successor, Clarence Cook Little, made no changes during his brief four years at Michigan.

Alexander Grant Ruthven became president in 1929, and led the University through the crises of the Great Depression and World War II. During his twenty-two year term, a private study was added to the house's northeast corner and Mrs. Ruthven obtained a glassed-in room for her plants. The Ruthvens introduced a tradition of hosting teas for students and other members of the community.

When Harlan Hatcher arrived in 1951, he found the Angell-era plumbing barely intact. "One morning the water for my shower came down before I had turned it on," he later recalled. After getting the plumbing fixed, the Hatchers added an enclosed porch and flagstone terrace at the rear of the house. Finding twenty-two rooms ample for their needs, the Robben Flemings have made no basic changes on the house since they moved in in 1968. In 1970 the President's House became the first structure in Ann Arbor to be entered in the National Register of Historic Places. □

Horace H. Rackham
School of Graduate
Studies

"In these higher courses we are advancing to the scope and dignity of a true University and maturing the noble plans of the founders." In 1859, with these words, President Henry P. Tappan expressed his encouragement for the establishment of a graduate program at the University.

In 1935, under President Ruthven's administration, the University received a gift from Horace H. and Mary Rackham which included a building and site for the erection of a school of graduate studies and a substantial endowment for carrying on graduate work and research.

Thirty-two buildings on two city blocks had to be removed before construction could begin in May, 1936. Architects for the building were Smith, Hinchman and Grylls. The building was completed in 1938.

A semicircular, 1,220-seat ground floor auditorium and fourth-floor amphitheater are focal points of the building which also includes elegant study lounges reserved for graduate students, conference rooms, art galleries, and offices that serve community and collegiate needs. Bronze, marble, wood, and glass serve as appropriate background to the beautiful furnishings— Chippendale, Duncan Phyfe, and Queen Anne walnut and mahogany—many of them designed specifically for the building. It is an impressive and appropriate setting for concerts, conferences, and "advanced literary and scientific work," "in a most generous, unartificial and earnest spirit. . . ."

Today the building houses administrative offices for the Graduate School, which include admissions, records, minority af-

fairs, faculty research grants, Rackham fellowships, and administration of Graduate Record Examinations.

The Institute of Public Policy Studies and the Bureau of Government Library also have their home in the Rackham Building, providing interdisciplinary programs designed to prepare students for careers as administrators, policy analysts, planners, and consultants in the public sector. □

Constructed by the Department of Buildings and Grounds, the building, with its three stories underground and four stories above ground, is ideally suited for physics laboratory and research work. Inside the building, but on a separate foundation with separate walls, is a small two-story brick building, completely enclosed, planned and used as a sound laboratory for noise-reduction studies. □

Betsy Barbour House

Regent Levi L. Barbour, during his extensive travels prior to World War I, had come in contact with two brilliant Chinese girls whom he brought back to the United States with him and sent to The University of Michigan to be educated. Distraught when one of these girls died of tuberculosis thought to be caused by unhealthy living conditions, Mr. Barbour dedicated himself to building a women's residence hall to be named in memory of his mother. The residence hall was completed in 1920. Her favorite rocker still sits in the small first floor reception room of this lovely home for 119 women on campus.

The convenient location and the home-like atmosphere make Betsy Barbour House a popular women's residence. □

Residential Buildings

Martha Cook Building

Among the University's most beautiful structures are those donated by alumnus William W. Cook (1882). His gifts to the University, including the Law Quadrangle, totaled sixteen million dollars. Ironically, he never saw any of them; he was a victim of tuberculosis and could not travel to see the buildings his generosity and meticulous care had created.

The Martha Cook Building, named in honor of his mother, was opened to residents in September, 1915. Since that time, more than six thousand women have shared the gracious accommodations and friendly spirit that are so much a part of life at Martha Cook. Architecturally reminiscent of the late English Gothic and early Renaissance periods, this building, like the Clements Library, reflects the tendency at that time to model academic buildings after European structures. Architects York and Sawyer of New York designed the building.

Particular attention was given to ceiling treatments in the spacious common rooms. The Red

Room displays a vaulted ceiling and plaster frieze reproduced from the existing "wagon head ceiling" in the library of the Castleton Manor House built in England between 1603 and 1614. The Gold Room ceiling was cast from original models in Sir Paul Pindar's home at Bishopgate, England. This ceiling is one of the best examples of plaster work of the early sixteenth century. In the dining hall, a furred beamed ceiling exemplifies the best Tudor style workmanship.

Seeking an atmosphere conducive to "the charm and grace and principles of cultured American womanhood," Cook created an ambiance of unabashed femininity with the installation of a full-sized replica of Venus de Milo as the focal point of a long, cloistered gallery off the entrance lobby. Throughout the building, Flemish tapestry, butternut woodwork, Jacobean furnishings, and Ming vases contribute to the aura of charm and dignity. The bust of Mr. Cook above a paneled fireplace seems to keep a bemused eye on current residents who are carefully selected, with emphasis on scholarship and leadership. □

Couzens Hall

In June, 1923, the regents accepted a gift from United States Senator James Couzens of Detroit for "the construction of a building for the housing of student . . . and graduate nurses." In 1954, Couzens Hall was removed from the management of University Hospital and became part of the University residence hall system. □

East Quadrangle
(Residential College)

The Residential College, a four-year, degree-granting unit of the College of Literature, Science, and the Arts provides an innovative, interdisciplinary living/learning environment for undergraduates at the University.

Established by faculty approval in 1964 as a "college within a college," Residential College students themselves appealed in 1968 to the regents for the funds needed for necessary remodeling. The Residential College graduated its first class in 1971.

East Quadrangle offers an ideal residential center where students, faculty, and staff can work closely together in the classrooms, library, dining halls, and theater, as well as in the courtyard which is dominated by a majestic 150-year-old oak tree that has come to symbolize renewal of intellectual growth. □

Residential Buildings

Alice Crocker Lloyd Hall

This residence hall is named for Dean of Women Alice Crocker Lloyd. The six-story modern building was completed in 1949, designed to house women students in four interconnected units named to honor four women prominent in the history of the University: Sarah Caswell Angell, Alice Freeman Palmer, Caroline Hubbard Kleinstueck, and Mary Louisa Hinsdale. □

Mary Markley Hall

Mary Elizabeth Butler Markley (1892) was one of the first women to graduate from the University. This dormitory, constructed in 1958 and housing 741 men and 448 women, is named after her. □

Mosher-Jordan Hall

At the September, 1928, meeting of the regents, plans were approved for a dormitory to house 500 women. At the October, 1928, regents meeting, a petition signed by fourteen angry landladies of Ann Arbor and their sympathizers was presented. The landladies feared that their rooming houses would be emptied by the new facility.

The building, however, was approved and completed in 1930. It was named in honor of the first two deans of women, Eliza M. Mosher and Myra B. Jordan.

Today it is a coeducational residence hall ideally located near the central campus, recreational facilities, and Medical Center. Warm wood paneling and four fireplaces provide a friendly atmosphere for residents to live, study, and enjoy a wide variety of social, cultural, and educational events. □

Mosher-Jordan Hall

Residential Buildings

Helen Newberry Residence

Like Betsy Barbour House, Helen Newberry Residence, built in 1914, was a gift to the University in memory of Helen Handy Newberry, the mother of the donors. In this case, the money was given with the understanding that although the property was to belong to the Student Christian Association, the hall would be built and administered by the University. This arrangement was dissolved, and the University received full ownership in 1925. □

South Quadrangle

There are seven individual "houses" in this building, opened in the fall of 1951, giving students the intimacy of life in a small college and at the same time the educational and cultural advantages of a large university. Approximately 700 men and 500 women enjoy lounges, study rooms, a snack bar, and dining rooms. The houses have been named in honor of former distinguished teachers and scholars on the University faculty: Fred Manville Taylor, Moses Gomberg, G. Carl Huber, Francis W. Kelsey, Jesse Siddall Reeves, Fred Newton Scott, and Claude Halstead Van Tyne. □

Madelon Louisa Stockwell Hall

Within the right angle formed by the two wings of this dormitory built in 1940 is a semicircular section housing two dining rooms on the first floor and a beautifully furnished lounge on the second floor. Stockwell Hall—named after the first woman admitted to the University—now provides accommodations for 432 women. □

West Quadrangle

Just off Regents Plaza to the south, behind the Michigan Union, is West Quadrangle. It was constructed in two parts, the first and smaller portion was designed in 1937 by Lane, Davenport and Meyer. The second and major portion was designed by Stewart Kingscott and completed in 1939. The building forms an angular figure eight with two inner courts. Primarily residence halls and faculty offices, it housed 1,300 navy enlistees during World War II. □

Other Residential Buildings

Fletcher Hall
Henderson House
Oxford Houses
University Terrace Apartments

Alexander G. Ruthven Museums Building (Exhibit Museum)

The first interest of the University in a "Library, Philosophical Apparatus, and Cabinet of Natural History," as indicated in legislative acts of 1837, was initiated by the purchase of an extensive mineralogical collection in 1838. In addition, 3,400 natural science books were purchased by Asa Gray, professor of botany and zoology. Consider in this context that construction of the first University buildings in Ann Arbor did not begin until 1840, and the first classes did not meet until the fall of 1841.

Philosopher Henry Philip Tappan, who, as first president of the University was determined to create " . . . a centre of light . . ." in this "Northwestern" outpost, strongly supported the museums.

By 1876, the museum began a second period of growth, stimulated by the Beal-Steere Collection of 60,000 zoological and 1,156 botanical specimens as well as archaeological and anthropological materials. Obvious need for classroom, collection, and exhibit space led to the construction of the first University Museum Building, ready for use in 1880. In 1885, the Chinese government presented the University with material that had formed a popular exhibit at the New Orleans Exposition in 1884–85. Acquisitions like these, plus increasingly active interest from students and faculty soon pushed the bulging collections into storage space wherever it could be found. This pressing need for space was accelerated by the development of other natural history collections and the development of separate academic units.

It has been said that the year 1928 marked the beginning of a new era of opportunity and productivity for the museums. The present exhibit museums (renamed the Alexander G. Ruthven Museums Building in December of 1968), partially financed by an appropriation from the state legislature, was ready for occupancy in 1928 by the museums of zool-

Alexander G. Ruthven
Museums Building
(Exhibit Museum)

ogy, anthropology, paleontology, and the herbarium. The building consists of two wings which meet at one common point to form the entrance—a plan largely determined by the need to design quarters recognizing the difference in size and space requirements of the four different museums. At the entrance, two puma-like black terrazzo figures, the work of Carlton W. Angell, stand below an inscription of Louis Agassiz's words: "Go to nature; take the facts into your own hands; look and see for yourself."

The exterior stonework is buff Indiana limestone and maroon tapestry brick. Interior decorative motifs are principally animals, including mythological ones. Reproductions of heads of pioneer American naturalists are carved in relief on spandrels between the third and fourth floors, on the entrance facade, and between the pilasters which repeat the entrance motif of each wing. Walls in the lobby and along the main stairway are of polished Italian travertine marble, the floors of badger grey and Tripoli pink Tennessee marble, and the ceiling of molded plaster. The wrought-iron gates designating research areas were executed by Roscoe Wood and donated to the museum by Otto Hans. Each wing contains laboratories, research rooms, offices, preparation rooms, and exhibition halls.

This superbly functional building was the result of years of planning by Alexander G. Ruthven, who in 1929 resigned the directorship of the Museum of Zoology to become seventh president of the University. "Sandy" Ruthven wrote to his staff and colleagues then: "The Museum is not finished. It never can be. . . . My earnest hope is that it will grow and change with the times. . . ."

And so it has. Today, collections spill over to separate buildings, the Museum Addition and the Museum Annex. Each year, more than 100,000 visitors, including 50,000 school children, enjoy the exhibit museum collections, dioramas, planetarium, gift shop, and the Hall of Evolution, which are open Monday through Friday from 9:00 to 5:00 and from 1:30 to 5:30 on Sunday. □

Institute for Social Research

At the end of World War II, a group of pioneers in social research came to the University and started what was to become a world-renowned center for social research.

One of the largest active archives of social science data in the world is housed at the Institute for Social Research on Thompson Street. The original building, constructed in 1965, and its five-story wing added in 1976, are the work of architects Alden B. Dow Associates, Inc.

Unique clusters of offices around a central open space lighted by large window walls permit discrete areas for separate programs, but allow easy communication among staff members of a particular research area. Because stairs, elevators, and rest rooms are centrally located, less space is needed for hallways, yielding an extremely efficient use of space (74 percent)—a high ratio of net to gross space for an office building.

More than 400 staff members at the institute conduct scholarly research on problems which are scientifically important and are of major significance to society. □

Student Activities Building

Student Publications Building

"**The** completion of the Student Activities Building marks a new era in student participation at the University," . . . "an inspiration and a symbol of student achievement." The idea of a Student Activities Building (SAB) was not new in itself, but student leaders took the initiative to meet with President Hatcher and other University personnel to work out suggestions and plans for the building.

April 26, 1957, was dedication day, although the building had been in use for several months. Swanson Associates was the architectural firm which designed the building with its aluminum canopy and louvers accenting the pale red brick walls.

The SAB was said to be the only one of its kind found on any college campus. Certainly the cooperative effort of students and University administration to create a facility primarily for student activity needs is a rarity.

The building currently houses the University Development Office, Career Planning and Placement, visited by more than 400 students a day, the Admissions Office, the Office of Financial Aids, the Orientation Office, the Scheduling Office, the Housing Office, and the student radio station, WCBN. □

Editorial offices and printing facilities for the *Michigan Daily* are located in this building designed by architects Pond and Pond. The first publication edited in the building was the *Summer Michigan Daily* of 1932.

The first issue of *The University of Michigan Daily* appeared in September, 1890. It was a strenuous undertaking but it persevered, sustained perhaps by its lofty ideals expressed by one of its founders, Ralph Stone (1892), at the thirtieth anniversary celebration: "The avowed object of the *Daily* editors from the very start was to furnish the news . . . promptly and accurately, likewise to promote clean athletics and sound morals among the student body."

Currently, the *Daily* has a staff of 120 students and a circulation of 10,000 papers reaching 35,000 readers. It is published daily except on Monday.

Editorial offices for two student magazines, *Generation* and *Gargoyle,* and the *Michiganensian* (yearbook) are also in the Student Publications Building. □

Tappan Hall

This small, red brick building just behind the Museum of Art and west of the President's House was built in 1893 by architects Spier and Rohns of Detroit. Regents named the new "recitation building" in honor of President Henry P. Tappan. The structure has had a wide variety of uses over its long history, largely devoted to classes in the College of Literature, Science, and the Arts. At one time President Angell's class in international law was held there. The Schools of Education and Business Administration have both had use of the building. Currently it houses the Department of History of Art including classrooms, library, and valuable collection of 190,000 slides and photographs of great works of art. □

Television Center

In 1973 the Television Center moved into the remodeled Argus Optical Factory on the historic Old West Side of Ann Arbor. Today it has attractive offices, two main studios, technical and set design workshops, a repair center for campus television equipment, rental service for small-format equipment, and the capability of doing film and video work on location.

The University of Michigan pioneered the effort to serve the television audience by means of "telecourses." The project began as an experiment fostered jointly by WWJ-TV, the *Detroit News,* and the University. With the use of WWJ-TV production facilities the first program was broadcast November 5, 1950. More than 12,000 registrations from interested students were received in the first four years.

Between sixty and seventy shows produced each year, plus approximately 800 previous titles, are available to an audience of 15 to 20 million viewers. Shows are provided free of charge to Michigan stations and at a small fee to those outside the state. Over 400 programs produced at The University of Michigan Television Center are played over commercial broadcast stations each year.

The center is equally committed to the adaptation of video technology to teaching purposes. As an example, law students, since 1961, have had the opportunity to observe courtroom procedures at close range via a video connection between an Ann Arbor courtroom and a classroom in the University Law School one mile away. The arrangement permits observers to manipulate cameras hung unobtrusively from the courtroom ceiling. It was the first attempt at such a linkage anywhere in the country and has had a successful endorsement by law faculty and students. □

William Monroe Trotter House

Tuomy House

William Monroe Trotter was editor of the first black civil rights newspaper, the *Boston Guardian*. He and William DuBois founded the Niagara Movement, the beginning of the NAACP.

The old Zeta Psi fraternity house on Washtenaw Avenue became Trotter House in his honor on December 27, 1972. Remodeled with funds from the University's Martin Luther King, Jr. Scholarship Fund, the building now provides a setting where students can exchange political, academic, and social ideas in the pleasant lounge, kitchen facilities, dance space, and conference and study areas. □

Cornelius L. Tuomy bought this farm on Washtenaw Avenue, the "Middle Ypsilanti Road," in 1874. Soon after, he ordered an addition built in front of the small house already on the site. Generously styled with double front windows, the addition contained two formal parlors on either side of the central hall and stairways with several smaller rooms upstairs.

After Tuomy died, two of his children, Katherine and Cornelius W. (Bill) Tuomy, lived out their lives in the house, forming a partnership to develop the property and sell lots as an expanding city encroached upon the family fief. Now part of the urban streetscape, the old Tuomy farmhouse was given to the University, which furnished a few of the rooms in elegant Victorian period style. The Historical Society of Michigan is quartered on the first floor, while the Michigan Academy of Science, Arts and Letters occupies the rooms upstairs. Woodchucks live in the basement. □

WUOM, the University's 230,000-watt radio station at 91.7 megahertz in Ann Arbor operates 18½ hours a day, seven days a week, 52 weeks of the year from its studios on the fifth floor of the LSA Building. Construction began on the main transmitter and tower at Peach Mountain near Portage Lake in June, 1947, and the first broadcast was made one year later. WUOM programming is received at WVGR, 107,500 watts, at 104.1 in Grand Rapids. Together they reach a potential listening audience of approximately 9½ million people throughout southern Michigan as well as areas in northern Ohio, northern Indiana, and western Ontario.

WUOM is licensed as a noncommercial radio station and shares programming with the nearly 200 other National Public Radio stations throughout the country.

The station provides a professional model for students and other individuals interested in electronic media.

Via connections to Hill Auditorium, Angell Hall, Lydia Mendelssohn Theater, Rackham Building, and, during the sports season, to Crisler Arena and Michigan Stadium, WUOM broadcasts the entire football and basketball season, and a wide variety of academic programs throughout the year.

Support from many individuals as well as some Michigan businesses and foundations has made possible new equipment and improvements in the studio and technical facilities.

A tour of the studios can be arranged by calling the station. □

1. Michigan Union
2. Alumni Memorial Hall
3. Law Quadrangle
4. School of Business Administration
5. Assembly Hall
6. Center for Afroamerican and African Studies Library
7. School of Education Building
8. East Quadrangle (Residential College)
9. Martha Cook Building
10. William L. Clements Library of Americana
11. President's House
12. Harlan Hatcher Graduate Library
13. Undergraduate Library
14. and 15. West and East Engineering Buildings
16. McDivitt-White Corner
17. David M. Dennison Physics and Astronomy Building
18. Clarence C. Little Science Building
19. College of Pharmacy Building
20. Harrison M. Randall Laboratory of Physics
21. Economics Building
22. and 23. Mason and Haven Halls
24. Samuel Trask Dana Natural Resources Building
25. Edward Henry Kraus Natural Science Building
26. Chemistry Building
27. Alexander G. Ruthven Museums Building
28. School of Dentistry Building and W. K. Kellogg Foundation Institute
29. Health Service Building
30. Power Center for the Performing Arts
31. Rackham Building
32. Modern Language Building
33. Burton Memorial Tower and Baird Carillon
34. Michigan League, Mendelssohn Theater
35. Thomas M. Cooley Fountain
36. Hill Auditorium
37. First Congregational Church and Douglas Chapel
38. Betsy Barbour House
39. Helen Newberry Residence
40. James B. Angell Hall
41. Kelsey Museum of Archaeology
42. Extension Service Building
43. Student Publications Building
44. Student Activities Building
45. Literature, Science, and the Arts Building
46. Administration Building
47. Regents Plaza

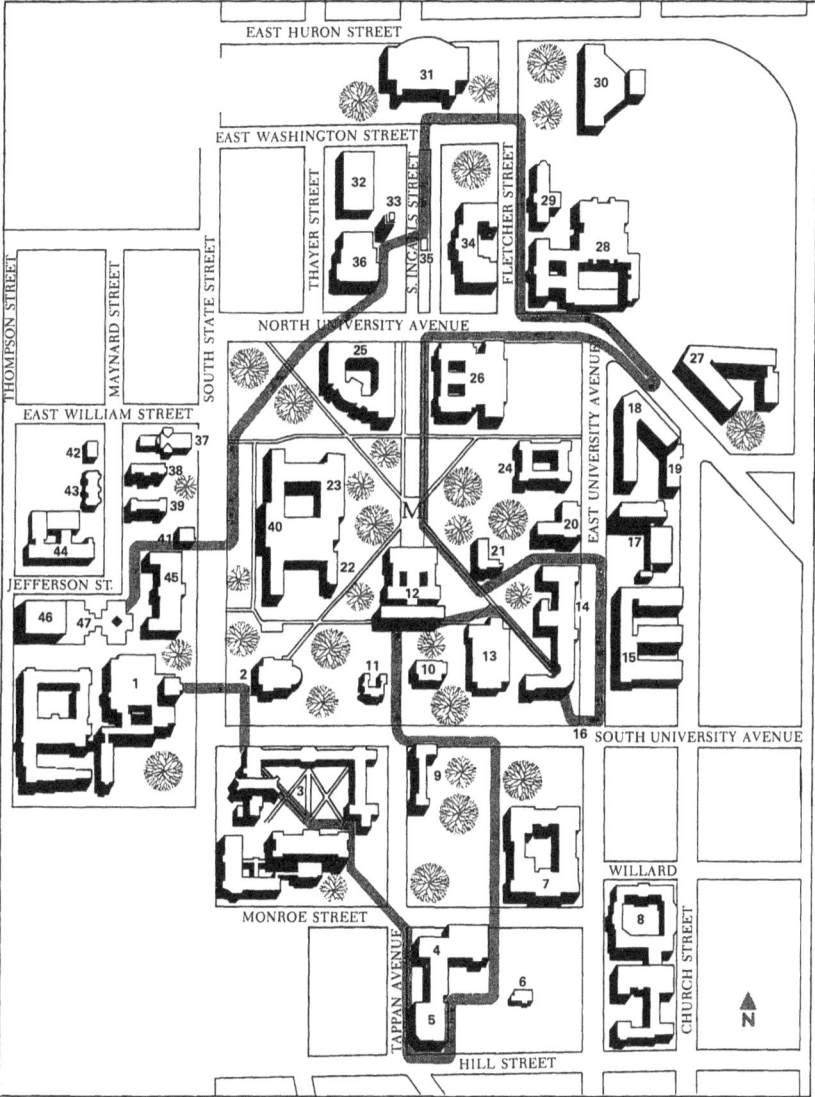

Stadium
Area

Stadium Area

Athletic Administration Building

Coliseum

Completed in 1955, the Athletic Administration Building provides quarters for the Athletic Department, including the athletic director and his staff, the Ticket Office, Publicity Office, and the coaching staff. It was designed by Giffels and Vallet of Detroit and constructed by the Henry de Koning Construction Company of Ann Arbor. □

Purchased by the University in 1925, the Coliseum served for almost fifty years as the University ice rink for recreational skating and for the hockey program. After the renovation of Yost Fieldhouse to an ice arena, the Coliseum was converted for use as an intramural facility for tennis, basketball, and volleyball. The Sports Coliseum Building, along with the Central Campus Recreation Building, North Campus Recreation Building, and Intramural Building, can be used by students, faculty, staff and their families, and alumni and their spouses by purchasing a user pass. □

Athletic Administration Building

Crisler Arena
(Events Building)

The 13,609-seat Crisler Arena,
named for Athletic Director H. O.
"Fritz" Crisler, was the creation of
two architects, Kenneth C. Black
and Daniel L. Dworsky. The
shape of the seating areas and
the steel-trussed roof allows an
unobstructed view of the arena
floor from every seat in the building.

Opened in November, 1969,
the building is uniquely suited to
host a wide variety of activities. In
addition to athletic events, such
as tennis, basketball, and wres-
tling, pop concerts, commencement, and special convocations
are held here. □

Intramural Sports Building

Matt Mann Pool

Located on Ferry Field, the IM Building was the first of its kind in the United States, erected in 1928 to provide intramural facilities for students, faculty, staff, and their guests. Earl Riskey is said to have invented the game of paddleball in this building, now used for competitive intramural sports, varsity competition, and state and national tournaments and exhibitions. The facility, renovated in 1976, is open Monday through Friday from 8:00 A.M. to 10:00 P.M.; Saturday from 8:00 to 5:00; and Sunday from 3:00 to 10:00. □

Named after Michigan's long-time swimming coach, the Matt Mann Pool was completed in 1957. It is the site of varsity swimming and diving meets as well as recreational swimming for students. It has seating for 3,000 spectators. □

Intramural Sports Building

Michigan Stadium

Nineteen seventy-seven was the golden-anniversary year for the Michigan Stadium, the nation's largest collegiate football stadium with a seating capacity of 101,701. In 1976 the stadium underwent a face-lifting, financed by bonds sold to alumni and friends of the University. The bowl-type structure, designed by Osborn Engineering Company, takes advantage of the natural slope of the land, so that the stadium rests in the soil of the hillside instead of being enclosed within concrete walls. The design of the structure also places the sides parallel to the playing field, bringing the spectators much closer to the sidelines.

More than 18,000,000 fans have watched the Wolverines in Michigan Stadium since the gates first opened in 1927. □

Wm. D. Revelli Band Rehearsal Hall

Track and Tennis Building

It was a Saturday. The Marching Band and the Alumni Band blared forth "The Victors." The occasion was the highlight of homecoming weekend, October 20, 1973—the dedication of the William D. Revelli Band Rehearsal Hall located across Hoover Street from Wines Field, where the 235-member Marching Band practices.

The building houses offices, a music library, storage rooms, and a rehearsal hall large enough to seat the entire band.

The Kresge Foundation and alumnus Ernest A. Jones, former band member and conductor, were donors of gifts that, with other contributions from alumni and friends of the University, funded construction of the building.

The building is named in honor of Professor Emeritus William D. Revelli, band conductor for thirty-eight years. Revelli was responsible for the national recognition of The University of Michigan bands both in the concert hall and on the football field. ☐

Indoor facilities for track, tennis, and baseball are available in the Track and Tennis Building built in 1974 to replace the former Yost Fieldhouse. The building, which has an artificial composition floor in contrast to dirt floors of earlier fieldhouses, seats 2,000 spectators for track and tennis matches. It is also used extensively by the general student body and faculty for jogging and tennis. ☐

University Golf Course

Women's Athletic Building

Two separate purchases of land, 112 acres in 1928 and another 15 acres in 1936, are the basis for the 18-hole golf course designed by Alister Mackenzie. The course first opened in 1931 and measures 6,865 yards for championship play and 6,425 yards for regular play.

The clubhouse was designed by Loree and Sirrine of Ann Arbor.

The golf course is open to all students, members of the M Club, faculty, staff, alumni, and their guests. Special arrangements can be made for outside groups who wish to use the facilities. □

Since 1976, administrative offices for the Women's Athletic Program have been located in the Old Athletic Administration Building which formerly housed the Intercollegiate Athletic Department. The structure is one of several buildings completed in 1912 at the time of the enlargement of Ferry Field. The former Women's Athletic Building was razed in 1974 to make room for the Central Campus Recreation Building. □

Yost Ice Arena

Yost Ice Arena, designed by Smith, Hinchman and Grylls and built in 1924, was the first of the three structures on Ferry Field. Seats for 7,500 spectators line the sides.

The building was named for Fielding H. Yost, football coach who had been with The University of Michigan since 1901. It was he who coined the name "field house." The building was constructed as a covered playing field which was large enough to permit room for a seventy-five-yard dash down the center.

The building was renovated in 1973 and is used now as an 8,000-seat hockey arena. □

North
Campus

North Campus

Art and Architecture Building

The School of Art and the College of Architecture and Urban Planning share this visually exciting building designed by Swanson Associates and completed in 1974. Built in the shape of a large open square with extended sides, it is faced on the back with rust-colored weathered steel. Large expanses of glass and the brick laid in Flemish Bond, a pattern very seldom seen in new buildings, create interesting textural differences. The open court in the center is floored with wood and serves as a showcase for metal and wooden sculptures. Long interior corridors become balconies on two sides of the building. Both occupying units share the Jean Paul Slusser Gallery where temporary exhibits are open to the public from 9:00 to 4:00 weekdays. □

To meet the challenge of ever-increasing computer use, the regents approved a North Campus site for construction of a new Computing Center in June, 1968. Designed by the architectural firm of Tarapata, MacMahon and Paulsen, construction of the building was completed in March, 1971. The interior space is entirely free of support columns. Raised false floors permit easy access to computer cables, electrical services, and the 900 telephone lines that serve the building.

In a typical month, April, 1976, for example, 126,933 jobs were completed by the center. □

Aerospace Engineering Complex

Aerospace Engineering is the current name for a complex dedicated in 1957 as the Aeronautical Research Laboratory—four buildings, on Hayward Avenue east of Beal, which helped propel Michigan into the vanguard of space-age research. The Research Activities Building, an isolated structure, houses the High Altitude Research Laboratory. Largest of the three linked units is the Plasma and Propulsion Laboratory. In engineering, plasma is a term for high-

Computing Center

81

College of Engineering

temperature gases which become ionized or electrically conducting due to formation of electrons and other charged particles as the gas is heated. Study of the interactions of electric currents, magnetic fields, and plasmas has given birth to the relatively new science of magnetohydrodynamics. Propulsion laboratory researchers have investigated phenomena associated with colliding shock waves, gases burning at high pressures, and the flow of gases through turbines.

North of the Aerospace Engineering office building is the Wind Tunnel, perhaps the oddest-looking structure on campus. There are, in fact, three wind tunnels—two of them supersonic, the other of low velocity. The low-speed tunnel, a 336-foot loop inside the building, is filled with screens and vanes which eliminate all air turbulence, enabling study of the low-speed landing characteristics of high-speed aircraft. Sudden gusts of wind can be simulated by the "moving bump," a device which is pulled along the floor. The supersonic wind tunnels, used for testing rocket and spacecraft models, can produce wind velocities from 850 to 1,700 miles an hour. The battering gales last from twenty seconds to three minutes, depending on which channel is used. Dry air from a storage area on one side of the laboratory rushes through a channel into a vacuum chamber on the other side. The bizarre chamber consists of nine empty railroad tank cars, sans wheels, joined together on an enormous outdoor rack. The nearby dry air storage chamber resembles a giant mushroom. Its dome roof of plastic over mesh was sprayed on in situ in 1956. ☐

G. G. Brown Laboratory

Built in 1958 and expanded in 1964, the G. G. Brown Laboratory on Beal Avenue provides specialized teaching and research facilities for all phases of fluid dynamics and control. George Granger Brown, a dean of the college, spearheaded development of the North Campus engineering complex. The Magneto-Fluid Dynamics Laboratory was designed for advanced research and instruction in space-flight phenomena, high-energy storage and transfer, and thermonuclear energy. It has three units: electrical, nuclear, and hypersonic wind tunnel. Winds of hypersonic velocity (five times the speed of sound) facilitate research on space capsule reentry conditions. The electrical unit is powered by a two-million kilowatt unipolar generator which provides electrical energy equivalent to the normal load of the entire Detroit Edison Company, for study of the properties of electric arcs at high currents and pressures. Electrical engineers probe electromagnetic wave reflection and absorption by ionized gases to better understand communication technology. Nuclear engineers study processes and conditions leading to controlled fusion reactions, which may someday harness the energy of the hydrogen bomb for productive ends.

Attached to the G. G. Brown Laboratory is Engineering I-A, an attractive brick building, completed in 1975, and devoted to water resources engineering. This unit brings together several departments of the University concerned with water resources. ☐

College of Engineering

Chrysler Center for Continuing Engineering Education

The Chrysler Center, on Bonisteel Boulevard, was a gift to the University from the Chrysler Corporation. Architects of the bilevel building were Swanson Associates. Opened in 1967, Chrysler Center can accommodate up to 600 conference enrollees at a time; its purpose is "to assist engineers associated with industry in the state to meet their technological objectives." The center's summer conferences and weekend "state of the art" courses help returning engineers keep pace with fast-moving fields of knowledge. Facilities include a 300-seat lecture hall, four conference rooms, two demonstration laboratories, and offices. A central electronic control room beams closed-circuit television pictures to or from each of the center's five large classrooms. □

Mortimer E. Cooley Building

The first structure erected on North Campus, the Mortimer E. Cooley Building bears the name of a former dean of the College of Engineering whose wit and dedication to the engineering profession made him one of its outstanding proponents.

Cornelius L. T. Gabler of Detroit designed the starkly modern three-story structure, completed in 1953, nine years after Cooley's death at age 91. The building employed early modular construction techniques described as "almost 'Tinker Toy' in its interior layout possibilities."

In 1966 the Engineering College's Industrial Sciences Group (ISG) was established in the Cooley Building. A "client-centered management center for interdisciplinary problems," the ISG applies emerging technical discoveries to the needs of man-

Chrysler Center for Continuing Engineering Education

ufacturing firms too small to have research staffs of their own.

Planned as the nucleus of a growing research area, the Cooley Building is equipped with two lounges, conference rooms, and an auditorium named for Professor A. E. White, first director of the Engineering Research Institute. The Reverberation Room, actually a three-story building within a building, rests on its own foundations, structurally isolated and therefore unaffected by vibrations or thermal changes in adjacent areas. The room is devoted to acoustics and noise-reduction research. □

Walter E. Lay Automotive Laboratory

North of the Cooley Building is the Walter E. Lay Automotive Laboratory, opened in 1956. A two-story structure, the laboratory building contains nineteen testing "cells" where students observe turbine and piston engines in operation. In the soundproof cells, air flows downward from ceiling vents to floor gratings, carrying off smoke and fumes. The three cells housing turbine engines use from ten to twenty pounds of air every second to meet both engine and ventilation needs. The laboratory's structures section is a large, open area for the study of auto bodies and chassis. Here vehicles donated by auto companies are displayed in cut-away form, revealing inner structures of bodies and frames. In 1976, the Automotive Laboratory was named in honor of the late Walter E. Lay, a professor of mechanical engineering who conducted early research on design aspects of automobiles. □

Space Research Building

The Space Research Building, across Hayward Avenue from the Aerospace Engineering Complex, was built with funds provided by the National Aeronautics and Space Administration. A two-story concrete edifice with narrow vertical windows in a facade of light brick, the austere structure houses the college's Space Physics Laboratory which conducts a variety of sponsored research projects for NASA. The building was dedicated on June 15, 1965, by two of the University's astronaut alumni, James A. McDivitt and the late Edward H. White II.

Plans for reunification of the College of Engineering on North Campus call for construction of three additional buildings and renovation of another. The Herbert H. Dow Building will house the Department of Chemical Engineering and Materials and the Department of Metallurgical Engineering. "Building One" will contain seven more units, including administration. A building for electrical and computer engineering is also in the planning stages. The Department of Naval Architecture and Marine Engineering will occupy the former Cyclotron Office Building, east of the Aerospace Engineering Complex. The Cyclotron—and its neighboring office building were erected in 1961, and operated under federal contracts until 1977. A shift in funding priorities caused governmental support to be withdrawn, and the "atom smasher" was dismantled. The building remains, surrounded by a high earth embankment, shielded against radiation leakage from atoms which spin no more. □

Libraries

Bentley Historical Library

Do not let the serene and unpretentious exterior of the Bentley Historical Library fool you. Inside, clustered around the landscaped courtyard that is graced by sculpture specifically designed for the setting by Richard Hunt of Chicago, is a comfortable reading room and generous stack area. It contains a collection of what is generally acknowledged to be one of the nation's oldest and finest archives of historical materials.

National interest in local history and the more specific needs of the historical profession are met by the Library collections—a noteworthy plural reflecting the dual role of housing University records and state historical source materials. Materials range from presidential papers, manuscripts, maps, photographs, personal papers, newspapers, and a variety of broadsides, such as political campaign posters and advertisements, to the crudely written journals of early Michigan businesses, such as the frayed 1895 ledger of the Postum Company with entries by C. W. Post. They are used by researchers from every major university in the United States and from more than twenty-four foreign nations.

Of the funds needed for construction and furnishing of the building, named in honor of the late congressman and regent Alvin M. Bentley of Owosso, half was a gift from his widow Arvella. Remaining funding was provided through numerous private gifts.

Among the library's outstanding collections are those relating to nineteen Michigan governors and public officials, including Arthur Vandenburg and Gerald R. Ford. The earliest gubernatorial collection, that of Territorial Governor George B. Porter, contains several letters from President Andrew Jackson.

Libraries

University of Michigan papers include materials from the founding of the University in 1817. War related records, an archive of women's rights documents, and collected materials concerning ethnic groups in Michigan are well represented. Perhaps the single most important collection is on the prohibition movement of the nineteenth and first quarter of the twentieth centuries.

All printed and audio-visual materials are available to serious researchers at the library from Monday through Friday, between 8:30 and 5:00 P.M. as well as Saturday morning from Labor Day to Memorial Day.   □

Gerald R. Ford Library

Papers of former United States President Gerald R. Ford will be housed in a library to be constructed adjoining the Bentley Library on the North Campus. The library will contain 20 million manuscript pages of documents from his long career as congressman, vice-president, and president of the United States. In addition, published and audio-visual materials, as well as memorabilia, will be available to scholars.   □

School of Music

Earl V. Moore Building

Eero Saarinen was the architect for this structure believed to be "the most modern and best equipped facility for teaching music on any university campus in the United States." Dedication ceremonies on September 19, 1964, culminated a forty-year effort to obtain such a facility. Musical activities and instruction which had previously taken place in thirteen different campus locations were joined in one building.

In its new building, the School of Music has numerous faculty offices, practice rooms, teaching studios, multi-purpose classrooms, and recital and rehearsal halls that utilize 250 pianos and 12 pipe organs. Tuning, adjusting, and overhauling these instruments is a full-time occupation for three staff members and the students who assist them.

Among the resources of the 55,000-volume music library are those in the former Stellfeld Collection. This collection of books, periodicals, music manuscripts, and photostats represents the lifetime collection of noted Belgian jurist, J. A. Stellfeld.

Both interior and exterior walls are brick, with classrooms and certain studios on the main level employing a second-floor slab "floated" on fiberglass or springs over the structural, concrete supporting slab. This design isolates these studios, making them soundproof.

The wooded hills of North Campus and the small reflecting pool at the back of the structure complement and enhance Saarinen's design. ☐

Frederick Stearns Building

Originally built as a fraternity house for Zeta Beta Tau, the modern quad-level structure now designated the Frederick Stearns Building was purchased for the

Earl V. Moore Building

School of Music

School of Music in 1972 to more adequately house the Stearns Collection of Musical Instruments. The Stearns Building also houses the Eva Jessye Afro-American Music Collection, offices for the School of Music faculty, and a beautiful small recital hall named for Calvin B. Cady, first instructor of music at the University in 1876. Excellent acoustics in this small room provide an intimate setting for informal concerts and individual recitals.

The Stearns Collection was a gift of approximately 500 instruments personally collected by Frederick Stearns (1831–1907).

The collection is intended to illustrate the evolution of musical instruments through several centuries and to represent "all classes, genera, and species." Some of the items are generally considered to be freaks and curiosities, a fact which Stearns himself acknowledged. But the collection achieves its objective. Primitive types and brass and woodwind groups are particularly well represented. J. P. Barnum once owned the most popular piece, an automated figure playing a clarinet. It was silenced long ago by a fire which destroyed Barnum's Museum.

In 1974, Dr. Eva Jessye, choral conductor of the 1935 premiere of George Gershwin's "Porgy and Bess," donated her collection of Afro-American musical materials including original manuscripts, plays, opera scores, recordings, books, and photographs to serve as the nucleus for future acquisitions of black music and related arts. Included in the collection are books, programs, tapes, and more than 200 copies of twentieth-century music with special emphasis on jazz and band arrangements by Duke Ellington.

The Stearns Collection of Musical Instruments may be viewed Monday through Friday from 1:00 to 4:30. The Eva Jessye Collection is open Monday through Friday from 9:30 to 1:30. □

North Campus
Commons

This building at the corner of Murfin and Bonisteel avenues serves as the North Campus counterpart to the Michigan Union and League. The structure was designed by Swanson Associates. On two levels, the offices, lounges, and dining facilities serve students, staff, and faculty. Art exhibits often hang in the main lobby area. In May, 1965, the senior class of 1961 presented to the University the bronze sculpture "Onus," located on the exterior entrance terrace. An original wooden wall decoration consisting of a large Viking ship and four ornamental shields hangs in the Viking Room. It was a gift of the architects. □

Phoenix Memorial Laboratory

Research Administration Building

The problems in accommodating large amounts of radioactive materials prompted efforts toward construction of a laboratory in which the potentially hazardous research could be done. The laboratory, constructed for the Michigan Memorial Phoenix Project, is a memorial to students and alumni who died in World War II. Created in May, 1948, by action of the regents, the purpose of the project is to encourage teaching and research on peacetime uses of nuclear energy. Early research support was provided to Donald Glaser for testing the basic principles which led to his invention of the bubble chamber, for which he was awarded the Nobel Prize in physics in 1960.

Architect Cornelius Gabler of Detroit created the three-story building of reinforced concrete, brick, and glass. A greenhouse with a unique inverted-V roof design extends the southwest corner of the main building.

The laboratory itself, completed in 1955, houses a cobalt-60 source, two hot caves, and laboratories equipped for isotope research. In conjunction with the adjoining Ford Nuclear Reactor, a two-megawatt–open-pool research reactor, the buildings provide radiation research facilities unequalled in the United States.

Tours of the reactor and radiation laboratories are available on request (764–6220) Monday through Friday from 8:00 to 5:00. Visitors should not overlook a large silk brocade portraying a Phoenix bird in the main lobby, a gift from the Institute for Chemical Research at Kyoto University, Kyoto, Japan. □

The Research Administration Building on North Campus houses three separate groups that provide services for research programs of nearly $80 million per year. This program—truly a national resource—is consistently ranked in the top five in the nation in the receipt of outside funds to support research.

The Division of Research Development and Administration (DRDA) is the administrative organization of the vice-president for research. It assists faculty members with all aspects of seeking support for research and administers the project grants. The DRDA project representatives act as the University's liaison with sponsoring agencies. Other DRDA groups have responsibility for program development, publications, and various administrative and support services.

The Business Office has several branches in the building devoted to business services specifically for sponsored research. These include Research Accounting, Sponsored Research Purchasing, Property, Travel Audit, and Timekeeping.

The Federal Government Resident Auditors maintain an office in the building. They are responsible for the continuing audit of federally sponsored projects. □

Residential Buildings

A variety of housing meeting the needs of both single and married students is available on the North Campus.

Baits Housing

Opened in the fall of 1966 and named after former Regent Vera B. Baits, these two units (Baits I and II) represent a new and progressive approach in housing. It offers an independent living situation with privileges and responsibilities consistent with the class level of the residents. The building was designed by Swanson Associates to house 1,200 students in ten different buildings. □

Bursley Hall

Named after former Dean of Students Joseph A. Bursley, this structure, opened in 1967, houses 1,200 students in two wings: 600 male students in one and 600 females in the other. Bursley Commons, in the center of the building, contains dining facilities, recreation areas, and library. Bursley Hall was designed by Swanson Associates. □

Other

Northwood Apartments

Baits Housing

Institute of Science and Technology

National concern following the launching of the Russian Sputnik in October, 1957, prompted an immediate appropriation by the State Legislature to enhance scientific endeavor on the Michigan campus. The Institute of Science and Technology (IST) houses laboratory facilities and office space for administering a variety of programs, including the Industrial Development Division which provides interchange between campus resources and state industrial research, the MERIT computer network with Wayne State and Michigan State University, the Macromolecular Research Center, the Biophysics Research Division, and the Great Lakes and Marine Water Center. Administrative offices for the Highway Safety Research Institute are also maintained here.

The award-winning design and construction were the products of the Detroit architectural firm of Smith, Hinchman and Grylls. □

Medical
Center

Medical Center

Medical Center

Opened in 1850 as the Medical Department, the University's School of Medicine and its ever-evolving Medical Center have long been fabled in story, if not in song. Lloyd C. Douglas, onetime pastor (1915–21) of Ann Arbor's Congregational Church, celebrated the single-minded dedication of the healing fraternity in his famous novel, *Magnificent Obsession* (1929) and its sequel, *Doctor Hudson's Secret Journal* (1939). Both contain recognizable references to hospitals and other locales in Ann Arbor and Detroit.

The old twenty-building Medical School and teaching hospital which Douglas knew had changed drastically by the time his book appeared. Founded in 1869 in a converted faculty dwelling, University Hospital—the first University Hospital in the world—took a dramatic leap forward in 1925 with completion of the mammoth building at the end of Observatory Street. During the succeeding half-century, other buildings were erected over forty-one hillside acres as the Medical Center grew, keeping abreast of rapid developments in medical knowledge and technology. From the beginning, all units of the Medical Center (a collective name adopted in 1958) have combined clinical, teaching, and research functions.

In addition to their role in patient care and research, the twenty-four buildings of today's Medical Center support one of the largest programs for interns and residents in the United States. Under guidance from faculty physicians, six hundred doctors-in-training staff the University Hospital, the Veterans' Administration Hospital adjoining North Campus, and Wayne County General Hospital in Detroit, while partially staffing St. Joseph Mercy Hospital in Ann Arbor and fourteen other affiliated institutions in Detroit, Grand Rapids, Kalamazoo, and other Michigan cities.

The Medical Center's clinical facilities in Ann Arbor accept patients on a referral basis, receiving difficult and unusual cases from all over Michigan. Medical students and their teachers observe a broad range of injuries and pathological conditions. Treatment occasionally results in medical and surgical innovations. For example, the Stryker Frame, used in turning victims of burns and spinal injuries, was developed at University Hospital by Dr. Homer Stryker (1925M). Hip fractures, common among elderly patients, are mended with the help of the Badgley Pin, named for the late Dr. Carl E. Badgley of the Medical School faculty. Probing medicine's frontiers, surgeons transplanted six hearts at University Hospital during the dramatic operation's experimental phase. In 1968 the first heart transplant in Michigan was performed here.

Replacement is imminent for the general University Hospital, now over fifty years old and structurally irretrievably obsolescent. It was in fact declared obsolete in 1955, but a multimillion-dollar renovation program begun then held the building together for another twenty years. Cost of a replacement building has been estimated at $150 million, which will make it the most expensive public structure in the state, a record now held by the University's School of Dentistry. □

Lawrence D. Buhl Research Center for Human Genetics

Children's Psychiatric Hospital

The Center for Human Genetics is devoted to scientific investigation of the mysteries of inherited disorders. Among the investigations in progress are the genetics of tumor viruses, genetic studies of mammalian cells in culture, genetics of the red blood cell, protein evolution, the genetic control of protein synthesis and the mysteries of inherited disorders in humans. Its building on Catherine Street was designed by the Chicago architectural firm of Holabird and Root, and funded by a gift from the Lawrence De-Long and Cora Peck Buhl Fund of Detroit, matched by federal dollars. It was completed in 1964. □

Extensive use of color brightens the interior of this four-ward, 200-bed residence for disturbed youngsters seven to fourteen years old. Remedial and corrective rather than custodial, the program here aims at providing happy home surroundings for children in small groups as a background for therapy. Each floor has its own kitchenette for a family-dinner atmosphere, large and small playrooms for active and quiet games, and a group therapy room for special evening activities. The building has its own school, as well as a gymnasium, swimming pool, and 100-seat auditorium equipped for movies and for plays in which the children themselves take part.

Opened in 1956, Children's Psychiatric Hospital was designed by Swanson Associates of Bloomfield Hills, and built to be indestructible, with "slam-proof" doors, tiled walls, shielded windows, and other features intended to absorb inevitable displays of temper. □

Kresge Medical
Research Building I

The low, linear profile of the Kresge Medical Research Building, dedicated in 1954, foreshadowed the utilitarian, but exceedingly flexible, architectural design of its later neighbors in the teaching and research group of the Medical Center buildings. Rooms are divisible into small units, and may also be combined to form larger laboratories as changing needs and programs dictate. Giffels and Vallet, Inc., of Detroit, and Skidmore, Owings and Merrill of New York were the project's architects and engineers. Construction began while the Outpatient Building (which they also designed) was still under construction. The five-story building was made possible by a grant from the S. S. Kresge Foundation.

Major research facilities in the original Kresge Building and its south-side additions—twin structures known as Kresge Medical Research II and the Kresge Hearing Research Institute—include special laboratories in dermatology, intestinal diseases, hypertension, metabolic and endocrine disorders, arthritis, anticoagulants, allergy, nervous system research, isotope studies, cancer serology, surgical techniques, immunology, kidney function, toxicology, and acoustics. The electroencephalography (brain-wave recording) laboratories are room-sized copper boxes, whose metal shielding eliminates electrostatic interference.

Animals, of course, perform a critical role in medical research. Animal quarters on Kresge's top level are air-conditioned, with easily cleaned tile floors and walls. Cages are washed and sterilized automatically. □

A. Alfred Taubman Medical Library

Like other divisions of the University Library system, the library supports the teaching and research programs of its constituency. Unlike most disciplines, however, medicine is a case-focused science, so the library fills an additional role in providing specific data for patient treatment and care. A MEDLINE terminal, connected to a computerized data retrieval system at the National Library of Medicine in Bethesda, Maryland, performs time-saving bibliographic searches on medical subject areas.

The library has a large (3,000 volumes) collection of rare books, including one-hundred incunabula —scarce editions produced before 1500. A valuable record of the early history of medicine and surgery, the books are consulted infrequently; to read them, a scholar must know Latin and Greek.

The groundbreaking ceremony for the new medical library was held on December 18, 1977. The building was named for A. Alfred Taubman who provided the largest individual commitment to assist in financing the building. When completed, it will house the books now located in the medical library attached to Kresge Medical Research Building I. □

Kresge Medical
Research Building II

Identical in outward appearance to the adjacent Kresge Hearing Research Institute, "Kresge II" was built immediately after the institute's completion in 1963. Another wing of the 1954 Kresge Building, Kresge II enabled expansion of medical research facilities hitherto confined within the larger structure. ☐

Kresge Hearing Research Institute

Another gift to the University from the S. S. Kresge Foundation, the Kresge Hearing Research Institute is a five-story wing connected to the Kresge Medical Research Building II. Architects of the cube-shaped institute building were Holabird and Root and Associates of Chicago. Buried two stories below street level and de-scribed as "the quietest building in town," the institute houses shielded rooms, vibrationless platforms, and echo-free reverberation chambers, which facilitate multidisciplinary research into the cause and treatment of hearing disorders. Functions of the organ of hearing are "so complex that their understanding requires the joint effort of engineers and physiologists, physicists and psychologists, biochemists and neurologists, pathologists and otolaryngologists," to cite from the list given in dedication exercises in 1963: "Rooms suspended within rooms, chairs and tables that tilt and whirl, colonies of dancing mice and the cooperation of whirling iceskaters all play their part in this elaborate integrated effort." ☐

Alice Crocker Lloyd Radiation Therapy Center

Medical Science Building I

Named for Dean of Women Alice Lloyd, a cancer victim, this building between University Hospital and Kresge Medical Research Building I is devoted to clinical treatment of cancerous diseases using teletherapy radioisotope units. Designed by Lansing architects Black and Black, the unusual underground structure has walls, floor and ceiling of high-density poured concrete. Of its twenty-three rooms, five are treatment rooms shielded with lead and concrete to prevent radiation leakage. The first cobalt-60 shipment from the Atomic Energy Commission was received in February, 1955, and the building was dedicated a month later. □

The first step toward geographical reunification of the Medical School and its hospitals was taken in 1958, when the dean's office and the Departments of Biological Chemistry, Pathology, and Pharmacology occupied this modern structure. This move, coupled with the School of Nursing's occupancy of one wing, inspired adoption of the name Medical Center to describe the mushrooming hillside complex. Teaching, research, and clinical work were placed in proximity for the first time since 1891.

Located on the lower level of Medical Science Building I is the Unit for Laboratory Animal Medicine. This unit is responsible for meeting federal standards in caring for animals used in experiments throughout the campus. □

School of Nursing

Occupying one wing of Medical Science Building I, this is a "temporary" location for the School of Nursing which formerly occupied cramped quarters in Couzens Hall. Nurses and doctors leaving Medical Science Building I can reach University Hospital through a long corridor perched on stilts, high above the traffic and safe from stormy weather. □

Medical Science Building II

Mental Health Research Institute

Completed in 1969, and designed by Holabird and Root of Chicago, Medical Science Building II gathered up the last of the Medical School departments formerly located on the main campus. The Departments of Anatomy, Microbiology, Physiology, and Human Genetics are located here. □

Furstenberg Student Study Center

The Student Study Center on the lower level of Medical Science II, was planned by William Kessler and Associates of Detroit, and won the firm a citation for excellence of design from the Michigan Society of Architects. Opened in 1974, and named for the late Dr. Albert C. Furstenberg, Dean of the Medical School from 1935 to 1959, the Study Center has the very latest in audio-visual and computer-assisted teaching equipment for use by medical, nursing, and other health sciences students. A wide variety of medical problems are visually displayed on screens in individual study carrels connected to a central computer. □

Located on Washtenaw Place at Catherine Street, the Mental Health Research Institute (MHRI) is a center for interdisciplinary research focusing on basic problems in mental health. Established in 1955, the institute moved into its own building in 1960, a structure designed by Swanson Associates. In addition to the usual offices, laboratories, and conference areas, the MHRI building has a library, hot and cold rooms for storage of tissues and specimens, a copper-shielded room housing electronic devices used in brain studies of animals, and a room with one-way windows allowing scientists to observe subjects without influencing their behavior.

MHRI's multidisciplinary research has probed the nature and causes of schizophrenia, the role of DNA in learning, uses of games and game theory, and brain functions and stress reactions in human and animal subjects. Data collected here were used in stress studies which preceded manned space-flight programs. "With the facilities at our disposal," say MHRI's scientists, "we can examine the normal and abnormal reactions of living systems, from cell to society." □

C. S. Mott Children's Hospital

Opened in 1969, Mott Children's Hospital is an eight-story structure designed by Albert Kahn and Associates. Most of the total cost was provided by the C. S. Mott Foundation of Flint. The late philanthropist Charles Stewart Mott, whose earlier benefactions had established the University's Flint Campus, was present at the dedication of this building. He was accompanied by two great grandchildren ninety years younger than he. Located between Women's Hospital and the Outpatient Building, Mott Children's Hospital contains over two hundred beds, a rooftop play area, the hospital school, the Neonatal Intensive Care Unit, and the James L. Wilson Laboratories for Pediatric Research. □

James and Lynelle Holden Perinatal Research Laboratories

Completed in 1972, the laboratories are connected to Women's Hospital and also to the Mott Children's Hospital—an ideal arrangement, since perinatal research is focused on problem pregnancies, genetics, endocrinology, and other medical factors affecting the baby's crucial first month. The perinatal period, just before and just after birth, has been called "the valley of the shadow of life." These laboratories, dedicated to dispelling shadows and ensuring a safer passage for infants into the world, were built with a gift from the Holden Fund of Detroit. □

Outpatient clinical services are housed here, with over two-hundred examination and treatment rooms, six lecture rooms, operating rooms, and radiographic and laboratory facilities. In the Nutrition Clinic, patients learn the dietary regimens required in treatment of certain diseases. Located at the west entrance, the Medical Center's twenty-four hour emergency service was instituted in 1953, the year this building opened. A five-story addition, designed by Albert Kahn and Associates, was built in 1973. The enlarged Outpatient Clinic is linked to the main hospital by a three-level bridge. The North Outpatient Building (NOB), an extension of the clinic facilities, is an older (1947), rambling structure perched on the brow of the cliff above the river. The Allergy Clinic, University Health Plan, plastic surgery, and medical illustration units are housed here. East of NOB is the Medical Center's Helipad, a site reserved for helicopter ambulance landings. □

Located north of the Huron River at 1000 Wall Street, with a sweeping view of Riverside Park, the Parkview Medical branch of University Hospital was purchased by the University in 1967. Formerly a private convalescent home, it is now a "therapeutic community" for University patients who are convalescent and ambulatory. The Scott and Amy Prudden Turner Memorial Clinic, serving as a geriatric clinic, was connected to Parkview Medical in 1976. □

School of Public Health Buildings

Dean Emeritus Henry F. Vaughan conceived the plan and raised the necessary funding from the W. K. Kellogg Foundation, the Rockefeller Foundation, and the National Foundation for Infantile Paralysis for the building designed by architect Lewis Sarvis and occupied by the School of Public Health in 1942. It was carefully planned to provide for patient segregation to prohibit contamination. Additions in 1959 extended the facilities available, but by 1965, some departments of the school were in eleven locations outside the original building.

Formal dedication of the Thomas Francis Public Health Building was held in November, 1971. The funds for the building were provided by the W. K. Kellogg Foundation, the United States Department of Health, Education, and Welfare, and University funds.

A bridge over Washington Heights Street to the original Henry F. Vaughan Building has proved to greatly improve pedestrian traffic between the two buildings. □

Simpson Memorial Institute for Medical Research

An old, unverified story recounts architect Albert Kahn's postconstruction tour of the ultra-modern University Hospital, which he had designed. Followed through the gleaming new building by University officials, the temperamental genius checked the view from a high south window and was enraged. "What is that building doing there?" he demanded, pointing to the clashing Renaissance facade of the Simpson Institute. His guides delicately informed Kahn that the institute's design and placement had also been a project of his firm.

The story may be apocryphal, but it is true that the Simpson Memorial Institute, an architectural throwback, resembles its enormous neighbor in neither scale nor form. However, there is nothing old-fashioned about the research which has been pursued behind these handsome granite walls. An endowment fund provides for the study and treatment of pernicious anemia and other diseases of the blood. In this building, researchers isolated vitamin B_{12} as a therapeutic breakthrough. World War II impelled research in the use of blood and blood substitutes for treatment of shock. Later the institute's investigative emphasis was shifted to leukemia, with compiled evidence pointing to a virus as the cause.

A gift to the University from Catherine Simpson of Detroit, in memory of her husband Thomas, the building was completed in 1927. □

Towsley Center for Continuing Medical Education

The Towsley Center faces East Hospital Drive, and is connected by a corridor to Mott Children's Hospital. Its completion in 1969 fulfilled a dream long shared by Dr. Harry A. Towsley, retired chairman of the Department of Postgraduate Medicine, and his colleague, the late Dr. John M. Sheldon. The building was a family project, financed by gifts from the Harry and Margaret D. Towsley Foundation of Ann Arbor and from the Herbert H. and Grace A. Dow Foundation of Midland, established by Mrs. Towsley's parents. Architect of the building was Alden B. Dow of Midland, Dr. Towsley's brother-in-law.

The two-story structure is in constant use for courses, meetings, and conferences. Every year, more than 2,500 doctors return to the University and to the Towsley Center to keep abreast of the latest advances in their fields of specialization. They assemble in Dow Auditorium, a 518-seat amphitheater; in the 144-seat Sheldon Lecture Hall; and in three large meeting rooms. Lounge facilities, a display room, and eight double guest rooms also serve their needs. Offices accommodate the Department of Postgraduate Medicine and the Medical Center Alumni Society which publishes the *Medical Center Journal.* □

Begun in 1918, University Hospital was labeled "Groesbeck's Folly" by political enemies of Governor Alex J. Groesbeck, and construction was halted when funds ran out in 1921. The looming skeleton was boarded up for two years before work resumed. Finally opened in 1925, the building was of poured-concrete construction, containing 1,200 tons of reinforcing steel covered with three million bricks that sheltered nearly two miles of corridors. Within days after opening, University Hospital was being called a "miniature city" and a "city of healing." Today's hospital complex has over four thousand employees, and treats about 22,000 inpatients in a year. Three times as many outpatients are treated yearly.

The thirteen-level building took the shape of two Ys, one pointing east, the other west, joined at the stems. This pattern, with open wards in the arms which could be monitored from nursing stations at the angles on each floor, was extremely effective, although the eighteen-bed wards proved less desirable in later years. Constructed of Indiana limestone, a separate administration wing faces Ann Street. The plan of University Hospital was copied extensively, as far away as South America and Australia. Several wards have since been divided into smaller rooms, individual floors are color-coded with compatible draperies, furnishings, and lively graphics.

The hospital's first addition was made when the building was only six years old. In 1931 two floors were added to the middle section (the surgical "wing") for a tuberculosis ward, including a light therapy room. Connected to the surgical wing on the north, the Neuropsychiatric Institute (NPI), erected in 1938, was also designed by Albert Kahn.

In 1940, interns left their rooms above the administration wing to be housed in a dormitory wing of their own, which sprang up north of NPI. The Interns' Home became the Clinical Faculty Office Building in 1975. ☐

Burn Center

The University of Michigan Burn Center is one of the finest critical care units for burn victims in the world. Its new treatment methods now save more patients and eliminate or reduce crippling effects of burn injuries.

The original Burn Unit was replaced in 1970 by a ten-bed wing in University Hospital that has allowed scores of patients to survive what previously were fatal injuries. The new unit, developed under a five-year grant from the United States Public Health Service, is a specially designed, self-contained facility with its own operating room, kidney dialysis facility, and hydrotherapy unit on the eighth level of the main hospital building. Designed to isolate patients from the ever-present danger of infection, the Burn Unit can care for patients for months, if necessary, without moving them. □

Completed in 1970 and designed by the Holabird and Root architectural firm of Chicago, the Upjohn Center is a northern addition to the Kresge Medical Research Building I. The Upjohn Pharmaceutical Company of Kalamazoo supplied the money to construct the center which houses laboratories for the development of medicines and the study of their uses and effects on patients in a clinical setting. □

Victor C. Vaughan Building

Women's Hospital

Erected in 1939 and intended as a residence for medical students, the Victor C.Vaughan Building saw service as a general undergraduate dormitory for both men and women students before its conversion to office use. Named for a former dean of the Medical School, the five-story structure now houses the Speech Clinic and the Center for Human Growth and Development, and a portion of the School of Nursing. □

Opened in 1950 on a site just east of the main hospital, Women's Hospital combines outpatient and inpatient service with facilities for the teaching of obstetrics and gynecology. Every year, hundreds of newborn Michiganders get their first glimpse of the world in the hospital's shiny delivery rooms. In addition to the large general nursery, several decentralized nurseries, adjacent to four-bed or private rooms, enable infants to maintain a close watch on their mothers (and vice versa) through connecting windows— an arrangement which keeps mothers and babies together from the earliest possible moment. A special room provides for the needs of premature babies; another for those of harried expectant fathers. □

Victor C. Vaughan Building

Other
Aspects
of
Interest

Other Aspects
of Interest

Arboretum (Nichols)

In 1906 Walter H. Nichols (1891) and his wife Esther Connor Nichols (1894) gave to the university twenty-seven acres of land between Geddes Avenue and the Huron River. That gift, plus permission to use twenty-five acres of adjoining city property and an additional gift of thirty acres from the Detroit Edison Company, provided eighty-two acres of land that is known as Nichols Arboretum.

The Arboretum was stocked with as many domestic and foreign plants as would acclimate themselves to Michigan weather and the variety of soils and growing conditions.

Today, Cedars of Lebanon, flowering fruit trees, and a peony garden delight the 60,000 or more visitors each year. A favorite spot during summer and winter for quiet reading, an occasional wedding and vigorous, impromptu sports, the "Arb" today might be classified more appropriately as a park. Still a cool, verdant refuge within the city, the Arboretum is open from 6:00 A.M. to 11:30 P.M. each day. □

Biological Station

In 1909 the first fourteen students to work and study at the Biological Station on Douglas Lake faced a gaunt landscape of blackened stumps twenty to fifty feet high—the charred remains of what had been a magnificent pine forest thirty years earlier. The crude laboratory facilities were modifications of a railroad grading camp built five years earlier, and the research fleet consisted of three rowboats of dubious buoyancy.

The students, however, wrote such enthusiastic reports of their experience that the director was persuaded to continue the experiment in biological education.

Today, it is the world's largest inland field station for instruction and research in biological science. The station occupies the 10,000-acre Bogardus Tract between Burt and Douglas lakes in northern Lower Michigan. Located in the transition zone between coniferous forests to the north and deciduous forest to the south, it is surrounded by a remarkable variety of forests, meadows, bogs, dunes, undisturbed shorelines (6½ miles), lakes, and streams. These immense areas of wilderness are unexcelled for teaching, learning, and research in ecology and field biology.

Three hundred residents may now utilize the 145 buildings that include the dining hall completed in 1976 entirely from private gifts. It was designed by Petoskey architect and Michigan alumnus David Trautman. Central to the teaching program is the Alfred H. Stockard Lakeside Laboratory completed in 1966. Twenty-five thousand square feet of floor space provide exceptional facilities, including an aquarium room containing a boat reservoir connected to the lake by a channel.

Douglas Lake is one of the most studied small bodies of water in the world. In fact, Biological Station personnel have published more than 1,600 scientific articles in scholarly journals. In addition, hundreds of reports have been written by advanced students and are on file in the well-stocked library. Five year-round residences have been added to the dormitory and cabin spaces, and as a result, more emphasis has been placed on winter research.

More than 6,000 students have received training at the Biological Station since 1909. Now, more than ever before, private, state, and federal agencies seek advice from the station. □

Chase Osborn Preserve

The Biological Station in northern Lower Michigan manages the Chase Osborn Preserve, a 3,035-acre tract in Chippewa County of the Upper Peninsula, located 300 miles from Ann Arbor on Sugar Island in the St. Mary's River between Lake Superior and Lake Huron.

In 1929 the land, with 60,000 feet of waterfront including all of Duck Island, was a gift from George Augustus Osborn and his father, Chase Salmon Osborn, Michigan's thirty-ninth governor and regent of the University from 1908 to 1911. Chase Osborn lived on the heavily wooded island in a log cabin, with his log-and-balsam-bough bed and concrete fireproof library of several thousand volumes. He is buried beneath a large granite boulder on the island he gave to the University "principally for research and instruction in the natural sciences and forestry." □

Botanical Gardens
(Matthaei)

In 1960 a gift from Mr. and Mrs. Frederick C. Matthaei, Sr., made possible the location of the Botanical Gardens on Dixboro Road. Experimentation on pharmacological and hallucinogenic plants is still carried out. The Medicinal and Herb Garden includes many of the classical species such as belladonna, digitalis, and the castor oil plant, all of which yield substances still used in modern medical treatment. Many of the plants in the herb garden are used primarily for their flavor, such as basil and savory; others for their fragrance, such as lavender and lemon verbena.

The plant collections have been specifically assembled to reflect the diversity of world flora, to exhibit plants of economic and botanical significance, and to illustrate the varied adaptation of plants to their environments. Among the natural habitats found on the 250 acres are woodlands, prairie, bogs, ponds, streams, flood plain, upland forest, meadow, and inside the conservatory, tropical, temperate, and desert environments.

Visitors are encouraged to follow four interpretive nature trails, enticingly labeled Woodmouse, Rifflebrook, Bobwhite, and Marsh-Pond.

The garden grounds are open from sunrise to sunset. The conservatory hours are 10:00 to 4:30 daily. The gardens are closed on Thanksgiving, Christmas, and New Year's Day. □

The University of Michigan-Dearborn

The Dearborn campus, one of three governed by the University's Board of Regents, was founded in 1957 through a gift of land from the Ford Motor Company and a gift from the Ford Motor Company Fund. Its 210 acres are located on a portion of the former estate of the late Henry Ford in the center of Dearborn.

From 1959 through 1971 the campus operated as a "senior-level" campus for students at the junior-senior-masters-degree level. The original facilities included a Classroom Administration Building, Student Services Building, Engineering Laboratory Building, and Faculty Office Building.

In September, 1971, the first class of 250 freshmen was enrolled, initiating new degree programs that now include management, electrical engineering, and education.

The historic former home of the late Henry Ford is the Fair Lane Conference Center that serves both campus and community. The fifty-six room structure was completed in 1915. It also houses The Pool—a dining facility in what was once Ford's indoor swimming pool. Both the conference center and The Pool may be rented by civic groups or individuals. The Pool is open for lunch Monday through Friday from 11:00 to 2:00. Guided tours are offered on Saturday and Sunday during the summer months and on Sunday only during fall, winter, and spring.

Approximately seventy acres of the campus have been set aside as an environmental study area, located adjacent to the Fair Lane Center on the western boundary of the campus. It is used extensively by University students and faculty for teaching and research in biology, limnology, environmental science, and bird banding.

A specially designed nature trail for the blind is located at the south end of the area, adjacent to Fair Lane Center. It offers a rope-guided path and cassette audio tapes for the visually impaired.

Open daily from sunrise to sunset, the area has several natural communities, including a beech-maple forest, an orchard, a man-made lake, and a meadow designed by landscape architect Jens Jensen. Guided tours are available. □

The University of Michigan–Flint

Saginaw Forest

C. S. Mott Memorial Building was the first home of the University of Michigan–Flint. In 1956 when the Flint campus was only a two-year college, the building was constructed by the late Charles Stewart Mott for use by the University, but with ownership by the Flint Board of Education. The building currently houses science facilities, faculty offices, and classrooms.

Ross House was donated to the University by Mr. and Mrs. Coleman J. Ross, Jr. in October, 1971, in memory of Coleman and Gertrude Ross, builders of the house. Resting on more than an acre of land, the five-bedroom house is the residence of U-M–Flint's chancellor.

The Classroom-Office Building (CROB), opened in January, 1977, is the first facility on the new forty-two-acre riverfront campus in downtown Flint. CROB is five stories tall and houses thirty-two classrooms, twelve seminar rooms, 150 offices, a library and four auditoriums. The building also contains a 410-seat educational theater utilizing a sophisticated lighting and sound system. The cornerstone of the new campus, CROB will be joined by approximately $50 million worth of new facilities in the next ten years.

Designed to house programs for the community as well as the University, the University Center will contain conference and meeting rooms, dining areas, swimming pool, counseling center, art gallery, and student activity and study areas. Scheduled for completion in 1979, its two-story glass facade will overlook the Flint River. University Center is being constructed entirely with private funds. □

Shortly after the creation of the Department of Forestry under the direction of Professor Filibert "Daddy" Roth in 1903, its need for a forestry laboratory was met by former lumberman and regent Arthur Hill of Saginaw. Hill purchased and then deeded to the University an eighty-acre tract of partially cultivated land located two miles west of Ann Arbor. Originally called the Saginaw Forestry Farm, by 1928, fifty-five acres had been planted in nine coniferous species and twelve hardwoods. Predictably, some species thrived while others suffered damage from disease and insects. Both successes and failures have been of value as a guide to future reforestation efforts.

A small stone cabin for the shelter of classes and work crews was built in 1915. It served as well for the popular annual camp fire and field days for forestry students. Total acreage now includes hiking trails, eleven-acre Third Sister Lake, and six acres of swamp around the west and south boundaries.

No vehicular traffic is allowed in the forest, a quiet, unspoiled retreat for students and casual strollers. The forest is open to the public year-round. □

Stinchfield Woods

A gift from Mrs. Annie Tillson Stinchfield of Detroit made possible the purchase of land for Stinchfield Woods in 1925. Total acreage, including additional gifts and acquisitions, now covers 890 acres. Within that area, Peach Mountain is the site of the University's broadcasting transmitter.

A short distance from the transmitter tower, a sawmill was constructed by students from the 1942 class of the School of Natural Resources. The first lumber was cut in the fall of 1947.

A large variety of game animals and birds live in the heavily forested woods. The area is open to the public year-round. Delightful scenic views of Portage Lake, Base Lake, and the Huron River make a visit well worthwhile. □

Mineralogy and Petrology of The University of Michigan

by E. Wm. Heinrich

Like most of the Lower Peninsula of Michigan, the campus of The University of Michigan is devoid of rock outcrops, being underlain by unconsolidated sands and gravels of glacio-fluvial and glacial origin which reach thicknesses of over 100 feet. To remedy, in part, this absence of natural exposures, there are several types of man-made structures and accumulations on campus. These include (1) a wide variety of building stones that "crop out" in the walls, steps, and pillars of a large number of campus buildings; (2) a modest spread of large glacial erratics and man-moved slabs displayed in front of the C. C. Little Building in which the Department of Geology and Mineralogy is housed; and (3) selections of rocks and minerals taken from the Mineralogical Collections of the University of Michigan that are on display in corridor cases on floors 1–4 in the southwest arm of the Little Building. Some additional mineral displays are also open to the public in the Alexander G. Ruthven Museums Building.

Some large rock specimens of exceptional quality and interest grace the front of the C. C. Little Building. Two have been mounted on pedestals on both sides of the west entrance. On the north pedestal a polished slab shows two generations of pegmatite dikes in transecting relationships, both intruding granite. The specimen appears to have been a glacial erratic probably obtained from the local drift. It may well have been plucked from exposures in the Upper Peninsula. The specimen on the south pedestal is a magnificent example of the giant garnets that occur at Gore Mountain, New York, where garnet has been mined commercially for abrasive for many decades.

The large specimen on the lawn is a slab of Dundee limestone (Devonian age) which shows three directions of glacial grooving or striations. Obtained from the Sibley quarry at Trenton, Michigan, it was a gift of the Ann Arbor chapter of the Daughters of the American Revolution.

Especially noteworthy are two specimens of contrasting ores which represent the bulk of the metallic mineral wealth that has been mined in the Upper Peninsula. One, a dark red banded iron ore with contorted layering, called jaspilite, rested for years in obscurity on a concrete pedestal behind Angell Hall from which it was toppled by "pranksters," and subsequently resurrected for display. It typifies the iron-ore deposits of Michigan.

Native copper ores of the Keweenaw Peninsula of Michigan are represented by a huge piece of the world-famous Calumet and Hecla conglomerate (possibly the largest such piece extant) from which the bulk of the native copper was obtained. The red slab is pierced by drill holes and stained green by secondary copper carbonates formed by weathering of the native copper that is dispersed between the cobbles and boulders of the conglomerate. Copper in the native form, that is, as the natural uncombined element, is a relatively rare mineral, and the deposits in Michigan are essentially unique.

The largest boulder resting in front of the C. C. Little Building is a glacial erratic of the most popular and colorful rock type formerly collected in relative abundance from the glacial drift—the famous

Mineralogy and Petrology of The University of Michigan

Jasper Conglomerate. These boulders were transported to central and southern Michigan from outcrops along the north shore of Lake Huron in Ontario. This one, which may be the largest ever recovered, formerly rested obscurely behind some bushes at the northwest corner of the central campus, whence it was abruptly and mysteriously relegated to the University's dump at the request of some un-enlightened bureaucrat. Saved from an unmarked grave by a persistent professor of petrology, it was placed in its present posi-tion with the aid of a crane, a "low-boy" transport and two fork-lifts, at a time when the ground was frozen solid.

Because campus buildings have been constructed for over 100 years and funded from both pub-lic and private funds, a diversity of materials and styles is repre-sented. Although this has resulted in architectural heterogeneity, it also allows geology students to examine a wide variety of build-ing stones, in a diversity of struc-tural usages.

Natural stone ("dimension stone") was employed for most campus buildings constructed be-fore the 1930s, after which time the mounting costs of construc-tion, and the rise in wages for labor required to quarry and shape the stones, combined to make the use of natural stone in publicly funded University build-ings economically infeasible and politically imprudent.

Two midwestern stones that are highly popular throughout the United States are also strongly represented on campus. One, probably the most widely used building stone in North America, is popularly known as the Indiana or Bedford limestone from its quarry locations in a belt forty miles long that extends through Bloomington and Bedford in south-central Indiana. These quarries, some of which are still operating, have produced at least 60 percent of all the dimension limestone used in the United States. The formation (Salem Formation of Mississippian age) has strikingly massive beds, thirty or more feet thick, so that huge single blocks have been readily obtainable. Three main color varieties were recognized by the quarry industry—buff, blue, and variegated, and further quality grades were designated on the basis of uniformity of color and texture; for example, select and super-select.

The Rackham Building is con-structed chiefly of Indiana buff super-select. Reportedly one en-tire quarry was exhausted in sup-plying the needs of this magni-ficent structure.

The columns at the front of Hill Auditorium also consist of Indiana limestone, attesting to its struc-tural versatility. William L. Clements Library is also con-structed mainly of this rock, and all three color varieties are to be seen in the walls of the old East Engineering Building.

Burton Memorial Tower is also built of Indiana limestone, some blocks of which have had a pecu-liar architectural history. The In-diana limestone is noted, among its other qualities, for its very low iron content. The architect, un-happy with the "new" appear-ance of the blocks, "aged" them artificially and rapidly by soaking some in a steep of iron filings.

A second popular building stone was the Berea sandstone, quarried in Lorain County, north-ern Ohio. It was utilized as the steps of Hill Auditorium. Alumni

Mineralogy and
Petrology of The
University of Michigan

Memorial Hall is the only structure on campus built exclusively of this sandstone.

One of the more unusual rocks on campus can be seen in the steps to the Graduate Library. Here the neophyte petrologist can examine Stone Mountain, Georgia, granite, characterized by one- to two-inch segregations of dark tourmaline crystals in a white feldspar-rich halo.

The Law Quadrangle is petrologically complex. The walls are of granite from Plymouth, Massachusetts, known to the quarrying trade as "seam-faced granite" because its variegated, iron-stained surfaces are largely natural fractures (joints). Indiana limestone is used as the trim around doors and windows and also has been shaped into gargoyles. The roof, constructed for permanence, consists of slate separated by a layer of asphalt from a substrate of four inches of concrete.

Some campus buildings also have utilized interior decorative stones. The Rackham Building is a marvelous example, with columns and wall panels of the finest Belgian "black marble." Travertine, a porous carbonate rock formed by hot springs, was incorrectly used by the architect for stair treads—a usage that has lead to inordinate abrasive wear.

In marked contrast to these examples of conventional stone construction is the Natural Resources Building consisting of shaped and fitted field stone. These boulders of glacial erratics collected locally were formerly very abundant in the glacial gravels but now have become very scarce. An example of modern stone utilization is the Undergraduate Library, the entrance walls of which display colorful crushed rock fragments stuck in concrete panels (terrazzo) which are then mounted as units.

Representative selections of rocks, minerals, and gems grace the hall cases in the C. C. Little Building. Of particular interest are those on the ground floor where some extraordinarily beautiful specimens are on display. Especially noteworthy are several cases of Michigan minerals; gemstones, both cut and uncut, from the Frederick S. Stearns Collection of Gems; Sicilian minerals from the Ph.D. thesis collection of the late Professor Walter F. Hunt; and polished marble slabs.

Displays on floors 2–4 are organized primarily for teaching purposes but also are available for public viewing. □

Trees of The University
of Michigan

by K. L. Jones

Andrew Dickson White, Cornell University's first president and United States ambassador to Germany and Russia, first taught history at The University of Michigan in 1857-63. In his biography he writes of first impressions of beautiful Ann Arbor:

But there was one drawback. The "campus," on which stood the four buildings then devoted to instruction, greatly disappointed me. It was a flat, square enclosure of forty acres, unkempt and wretched. Throughout its whole space there were not more than a score of trees outside the building sites allotted to professors; unsightly plank walks connected the buildings, and in every direction were meandering paths, which in dry weather were dusty and in wet weather muddy. Coming, as I did, from the glorious elms of Yale, all this distressed me, and one of my first questions was why no trees had been planted. The answer was that the soil was so hard and dry that none would grow. But on examining the territory in the neighborhood, especially the little inclosures about the pretty cottages of the town, I found fine large trees, and among them elms. At this, without permission from any one, I began planting trees within the university enclosure; established, on my own account, several avenues; and set out elms to overshadow them. Choosing my trees with care, carefully protecting and watering them during the first two years, and gradually adding to them a considerable number of evergreens, I preached practically the doctrine of adorning the campus. Gradually some of my students joined me; one class after another aided in securing trees and in planting them, others became interested, until, finally, the university authorities made me "superintendent of the grounds," and appropriated to my work the munificent sum of seventy-five dollars a year. So began the splendid growth which now surrounds those buildings. These trees became to me as my own children. Whenever I revisit Ann Arbor my first care is to go among them, to see how they prosper, and especially how certain peculiar examples are flourishing; and at my recent visit, forty-six years after their planting, I found one of the most beautiful academic groves to be seen in any part of the world.

Today the central campus is still adorned by majestic American elms planted by Andrew Dickson White and his students. Sadly, they no longer form "one of the most beautiful academic groves to be seen in any part of the world." Of the four original buildings only the President's House remains; but what congeries of brick, stone, and mortar have crowded out the grove, to mention nothing of the maze of concrete walks. Acts of nature, the Dutch elm disease, fire from lightning bolts, and at least two cataclysmic ice storms have taken a toll that no ecologist could have averted.

Of the ice storms, we have an eye-witness report in the late Professor Harley Harris Bartlett's diary, March 12, 1939.

Botany greenhouse about 1/4 smashed by a falling limb of the big elm tree that overhangs it. The whole campus is full of wreckage. [Being a Sunday, the Diagonal was roped off to prevent injury to pedestrians from falling "timber."] There has been no such damage to trees since the even greater ice storm 17 years ago, I think it was when I spent most of the night walking Robert Frost, who was in poetic fervor about it all. After taking him home the last time (we had walked home with the other 2 or 3 times) the street lights on Cambridge Road were all out and I fell into the sunken garden near the corner of Olivia Street, and couldn't get out, until about 4 A.M. [Frost's poem, "Brown's Descent or the Willy Nilly Slide" recreates this episode].

Ice storms shatter branches of elms in particular and thus expose them to fungal parasites. Some individual elms on campus have shown remarkable healing qualities. For example, a venerable specimen west of the old Physics building bears a fire scar from a lightning bolt which extends a good thirty feet up the trunk.

Southwest of the Library stands the bur oak honoring President Tappan. The Tappan Oak has been a meeting place for certain honor societies in the performing of initiation rites. For years, during each spring, fresh buckets of red-brown paint redecorated its trunk.

Ann Arbor is believed to have been set out, as a community of sorts, prior to 1824 in a bur oak clearing. Whether the half-dozen or so venerable oaks surviving on the central campus today are natural remnants of the bur oak forest or were planted by Professor White and his students is difficult to determine. A rare hybrid between bur oak and white oak stands north of Mason Hall.

There is a sizeable black oak south of Alumni Memorial Hall and two bur oaks on the grounds of the President's House.

Aside from the numerous elms —especially the splendid State Street row—and the oaks, there are a few other pioneers. Two lofty black walnut trees grow on South University Avenue near Alumni Memorial Hall. One wonders about the origin of the single specimen of Wych elm within the Law Quadrangle. This is not to be confused with the American elms which were set out in orderly pattern when the quadrangle came into being in the 1920s. The elms were transplanted as inordinately large trees —really choice acquisitions at the time, appropriate to their setting.

Sugar maples, which in autumnal coloration surpass all our trees, are represented today by few, if any, specimens dating back to the 1850s. Before the Diagonal widened and was encroached upon by buildings at its eastern end, sugar maples were numerous. A few older trees of this species occur near the Alumni Memorial Hall. The most symmetrical and vividly colored, though younger, sugar maple is to be found on the east side of William L. Clements Library. The rarer sycamore maple, gnarled and unspectacular, subsists near the southern corner of Angell Hall.

Another of the older trees is an ash, possibly an "English ash," located in front of the Graduate Library at the western corner. It is as tall as the elms and the Tappan Oak nearby. Having its lower branches removed, identification of the tree is not immediately apparent. This ash was said to be the remaining specimen from the first Botanical Garden which was located in the center of campus.

Trees of The University
of Michigan

Those of us who knew the central campus on into the Ruthven era will cherish memories of the gaily lighted yuletide firs embracing the Graduate Library steps. The trees were decorated a week before the winter holidays and greeted the reluctant students on their return to the "sudden-death session," two weeks of classes prior to the inevitable "finals" which then were three-hour examinations.

Trees of note that have come to maturity on the central campus since the erection of Angell Hall in 1924 include: *Gingko biloba* (maidenhair tree) in front of the Michigan Union; the horse chestnut—not to be confused with the buckeye—a familiar sight south of the steps of Angell Hall, particularly when its candle-like floral clusters are in full bloom; the piebald-barked sycamores on South University Avenue and south of the Michigan Union; the patient beech on the front lawn of the Sigma Chi chapter house on South State Street; the paired Austrian pines before the Law School refectory; the spire-like white pine in the north section of the president's yard; and the circular magnolias in the Martha Cook Building plantings as contrasted with the lofty one before the northwest entrance of the Rackham Building.

The maidenhair, *Gingko biloba,* is a botanical oddity, being a seedplant approximating the conifers but having leaves shaped and veined as the maidenhair fern. I have heard students point out this large, broadly spreading Gingko located in front of the Union as "the only one in the world!" That is not quite accurate. Gingko has had a long history on this earth; it has become recognized as a splendid tree for city planting because of its resistance to air pollution and ability to survive close incursions of concrete. The Union specimen had its upper trunk snipped off years ago when a construction truck hit a wire stretched across State Street. The Michigan League, not to be surpassed, has a younger but more typically shaped maidenhair tree planted north of the building.

The apricot tree of the Michigan League garden had to be replaced. A magnolia failed, but "October Glory" a cultivar of sugar maple reigns in its stead. The actor, Will Geer, who was in residence at the League in 1966 helped instigate a Shakespeare Garden with the apricot tree as its center. The tree sprouted from a volunteer seedling at the turn of the century along the fence of the Drake Rooming House, the site on which the League was later built. An account of the Shakespeare Garden done on the playwright's 400th anniversary was pleasantly recorded in the *Ann Arbor News* of October 20, 1966, under the caption, "Will Geer Gears Garden to Style of Elizabethans." He himself wrote of Ann Arbor's Shakespeare Garden, "There will never be an end to the making of gardens or to the playing of Shakespeare."

Mixed plantings have been introduced on central campus in the past quarter of a century. Whether by intent or chance this is good sense ecologically as it will obviate destruction by a specific parasite as befell the American elm. White pine, red or black oak, honey locust, and maples of considerable size were set out attractively in the cement-bordered mall east of the Administration Building. Low branching beech are tastefully

planted at the far corners of the
Literature, Science, and the Arts
Building where a specimen elm
shades the rear entrance. Redbud
has come to maturity, softening
the old face of Dentistry's Kellogg
Institute. Sweet gum, in its own
way, may compensate for the loss
of the cozy Camperdown elm
(umbrella tree) that was a convenient lingering nook near the
Graduate Library. Very plucky
rows of flowering crab give a
May-time touch to the long side
of Mason Hall and also to the
south entrance to the Michigan
League in sight of the geometrical
flower beds of tulips at May Festival time.

In the sealed mini-quadrangle
enclosed by corridors of Mason
Hall, lithesome birch display their
white stems to the hordes of students who have read of Robert
Frost's *Birches* but can never
touch these, let alone swing to
earth on them. Witch hazel, the
small shrub with clusters of yellow
flowers that appear *after* the
leaves have fallen and whose dis-
tilled sap from the bark yields a
one-time favorite rubbing oint-
ment, has stood very well along
the western side of the Kraus
Natural Science Building. The
graceful laburnums, with festoons
of yellow flowers, reminiscent of
the purple tree-wisterias once
fronting the Literature, Science,
and the Arts Building, have been
reduced to two slender trees.

Central campus is hardly the
academic grove of Professor
Andrew White's later years, but
it has the makings of becoming
one. ☐

Index

Index

Index

Index

Index

Illustrated Campus Map

OF THE UNIVERSITY OF MICHIGAN

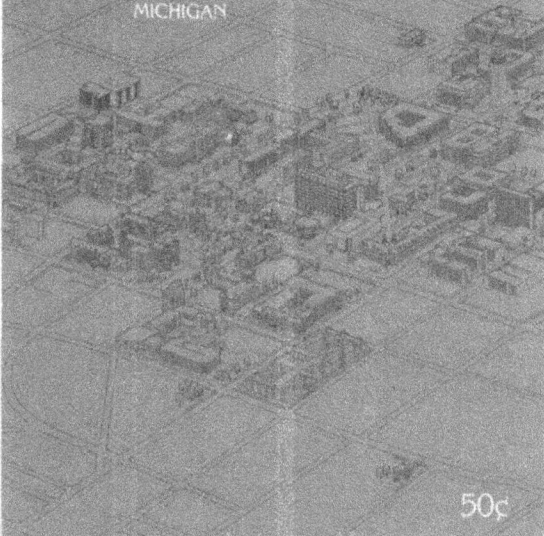

50¢

Published by
University Relations and Development
The University of Michigan
and sold by
University Publications Office

The purchase price of this map helps defray
the cost to the University of providing a comprehensive
guide to the campus.

Points of Interest at The University of Michigan

Landmarks

President's House —built in 1840 as one of the first buildings for the University, it has been placed on the National Register of Historic Places by the National Park Service.

Burton Memorial Tower — erected in 1936 as a memorial to former president Marion Burton, it contains the 55-bell carillon donated by Charles Baird. The tower is open to visitors on a regular schedule.

Michigan Stadium — the nation's largest collegiate-owned stadium is the center of attraction on fall football Saturdays in Ann Arbor. The largest crowd attending a single game numbered more than 107,000.

Michigan League — erected in 1929 in part with funds raised through the efforts of the Women's League of the University and alumnae groups throughout the country. The League cafeteria and snack bar are open to the public and private meeting rooms are available.

Michigan Union — originally incorporated as a social center for men, now houses many of the offices of the Office of Student Services as well as the Alumni Association.

Museums

Museum of Art — located in Alumni Memorial Hall, it is one of the finest University art museums in the country. A varied permanent collection is enhanced by a continuing series of special exhibitions. The museum is open to the public daily.

Exhibit Museum — the Alexander G. Ruthven Museums Building houses the University's Exhibit Museum which includes three floors of displays including the Hall of Evolution, exhibits of Michigan plants and animals, mineral and biological displays, and a planetarium, all open to the public daily. Also in the building are the research Museums of Anthropology, Zoology, and Paleontology.

Kelsey Museum of Ancient and Medieval Archaeology — is housed in Newberry Hall, one of the oldest buildings on campus. On display are works of art and archaeological specimens illustrating the life of the Mediterranean world and the Near East in antiquity and the middle ages.

Theatres

Hill Auditorium — is used for music and dance presentation, including the series of the University Musical Society and the annual May Festival, and for lectures and academic presentations. The gift of Regent Arthur Hill, it houses the Frieze Memorial Organ and seats 4,200 people.

Lydia Mendelssohn Theatre — is a 700-seat theatre constructed with a gift from Mr. Gordon Mendelssohn of Birmingham. It houses student and professional theatre and musical events and the offices of the Professional Theatre Program.

Power Center for the Performing Arts — is the University's newest facility for theatre, dance, and musical presentations. Made possible by generous gifts from former regent Eugene B. Power and his family, the 1,420-seat performing arts center has become a campus landmark.

NORTH CAMPUS

401 Aerospace Building, F-2
402 Art and Architecture Building, B-2
403 Vera Baits Houses, A-4
404 Bentley Historical Library/
     Michigan Historical Collections,
     D-2
405 G. G. Brown Laboratory, E-3
406 Bursley Hall, B-4
407 Chrysler Center for Continuing
     Engineering Education, C-2
408 Computing Center, C-2
409 Mortimer E. Cooley Building, D-2
410 Electrical Station, E-2
411 Engineering 1-A, E-2
412 Fire Service Instruction and
     Research Center, H-4
413 Ford Nuclear Reactor, D-2
414 Highway Safety Research
     Institute, K-3
415 University Laundry, M-2
416 Walter E. Lay Automotive
     Laboratory, D-2
417 Library Extension Service and
     Library Storage, D-2

418 Earl V. Moore School of Music
     Building, A-3
419 Naval Architecture and Marine
     Engineering Building, F-2
420 North Campus Commons, C-3
421 North Campus Recreation
     Building, D-4
422 Northwood Apartments I, II, & III,
     D-G-4
423 Northwood Apartments IV, H-J-4
424 Northwood Apartments V, J-K-1
425 Phoenix Memorial Laboratory,
     D-2
426 Property Disposition, N-2
427 Research Activities Building, F-3
428 Research Administration
     Building, D-2
429 Institute of Science and
     Technology, C-2
430 Space Research Building, F-3
431 Frederick Stearns Building, A-4
432 University Printing Services, C-2

Libraries

The library system of the University includes the Harlan Hatcher Graduate Library, the Undergraduate Library, 21 divisional libraries, 7 departmental and area collections, the Law and Business Administration Libraries, and these special libraries:

William L. Clements Library of Americana — given to the University by the late regent and alumnus William L. Clements, it houses the donor's invaluable collection of Americana upon which the University has continued to build. The collection includes books, newspapers, maps, manuscripts, and prints from 1492 to the middle of the nineteenth century. The library is open to the public.

Michigan Historical Collections/Bentley Historical Library — preserves, and makes available for research, manuscript and printed materials relating to the people and institutions of the State of Michigan. In addition, the collections offer rich resources for the study of the Philippine Islands and the American temperance and prohibition movement, as well as serving as the archives of the University.

Gerald R. Ford Presidential Library — now being planned on a site adjacent to the Bentley Library on the North Campus, will house Mr. Ford's Presidential, Vice-Presidential, and Congressional documents.

Where to Find It

Accounting Department, 3028 Administration Services, C-3
Admissions Office (undergraduate), 1220 Student Activities Building, H-4
Conference Department, Extension Service, 350 S. Thayer St.
Financial Aid (Student), 2011 Student Activities Building, H-4
Parking Operations, 411 E. Jefferson St., G-4
Personnel Office, 2031 Administrative Services, C-3
Purchasing Department (Central), 3025 Administrative Services Building C-3
Staff Benefits Office, 2030 Administrative Services Building, C-3
Ticket Office (Athletics Only), 1000 S. State, F-2
University Relations, 1028 Administration Building, G-4
Visitor and Guest Relations, 6044 Administration Building, G-4

For information about University programs and events dial 764-1817 (from 763 or 764 exchanges dial "0"). For recorded news briefs dial 763-1300.

VISITOR INFORMATION — Reception desks, lobbies of the Literature, Science, and the Arts Building (H-4) and the Administration Building (G-4).

North Campus

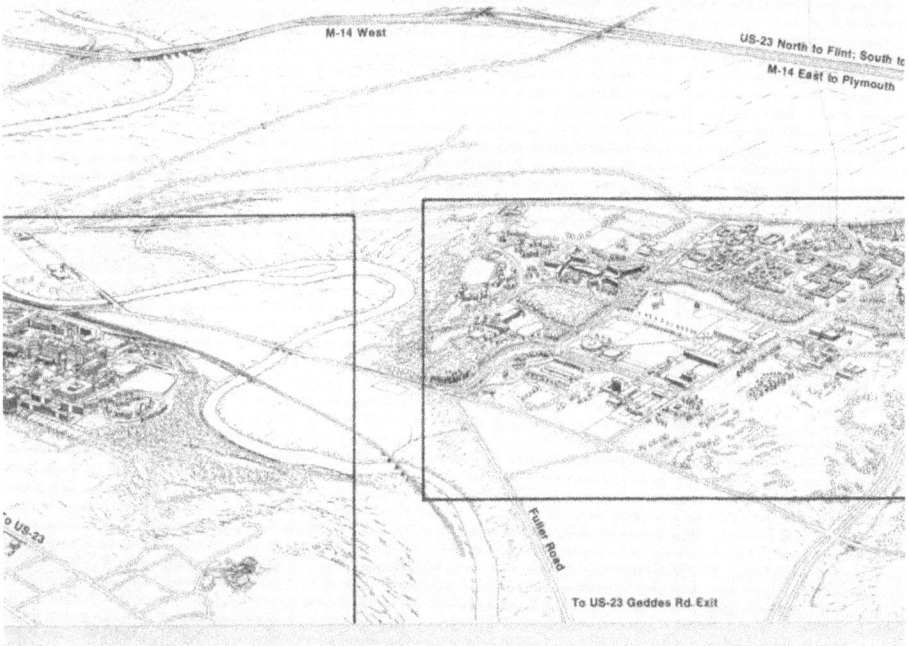

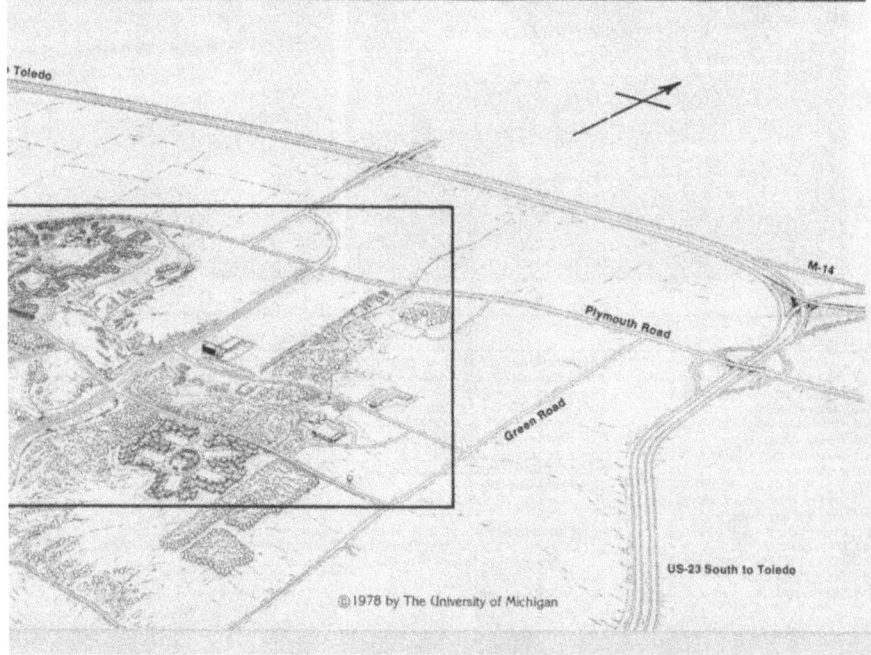

Welcome to The University of Michigan

In 1817 the Michigan territorial legislature chartered the Catholepistemiad of Michigania, the ancestor of The University of Michigan, in the frontier town of Detroit. In 1837 the University was reorganized and moved to Ann Arbor, where the original 40-acre campus had been proffered as a gift. That original site is the area bounded by State Street and North, East, and South University Avenues.

Today the University comprises 19 schools and colleges on campuses in Ann Arbor, Flint, and Dearborn. Related research and educational units include 31 centers, 13 institutes, 3 Bureaus, and 9 hospital units.

The University's fall term enrollment in Ann Arbor averages 38,000. Approximately two-thirds are undergraduates and one-third are graduate and graduate-professional students.

Education at Michigan can be measured from a strictly quantitative standpoint: approximately 10,000 degrees are granted each year. On the qualitative side: in the most recent survey by the American Council on Education, The University of Michigan had 12 departments among the top five and 23 among the top 10 in the nation.

The University of Michigan combines state appropriations with federal government support, alumni and other private support, and tuition. This combination of fund sources allows the University to maintain its high standards of excellence.

Particularly important has been the private support of alumni, foundations, corporations, and friends of the University, which has provided the vital margin of philanthropy that has helped Michigan achieve and retain its position as one of the ten leading universities in the nation.

About the Ann Arbor Campus

The University of Michigan's land holdings in Ann Arbor total 2,581 acres, much of it shown on these maps. The physical plant includes 202 major buildings as well as 220 Northwood Apartment buildings on the North Campus. The total plant is valued at more than $610,000,000.

The Ann Arbor Campus, which swings in a crescent through the city, is subdivided generally into the Stadium Area, the Central Campus, the Medical Center, and the North Campus. The North Campus area and a map showing the entire Ann Arbor area and the avenues of approach from the expressways that ring the city are on the back of this sheet.

The Schools and Colleges

Seventeen of the University's nineteen schools and colleges are located in Ann Arbor. Bulletins (catalogs) and other information are available at the individual unit offices listed below. Map references preceded by (NC) are for the North Campus map on the reverse of this sheet.

College of Architecture and Urban Planning, 2000 Bonisteel Blvd., (NC) B-2
School of Art, 2000 Bonisteel Blvd., (NC) B-2
School of Business Administration, 904 Monroe St., H-3
School of Dentistry, 1011 N. University, L-4
School of Education, 610 E. University, J-3
College of Engineering, 550 E. University, K-3
Horace H. Rackham School of Graduate Studies, 915 E. Washington, L-5
Law School, 625 S. State, H-3
School of Library Science, 580 Union Drive, G-4
College of Literature, Science, and the Arts, 500 S. State, H-4
    Residential College of LSA, 701 E. University, J-3
Medical School, 1335 E. Catherine, P-5
School of Music, 1100 Baits Dr., (NC) A-3
School of Natural Resources, 430 E. University, K-4
School of Nursing, 1335 Catherine, P-5
College of Pharmacy, 428 Church St., L-4
School of Public Health, 109 S. Observatory, P-4
School of Social Work, 1065 Frieze Bldg., E. Washington, K-5

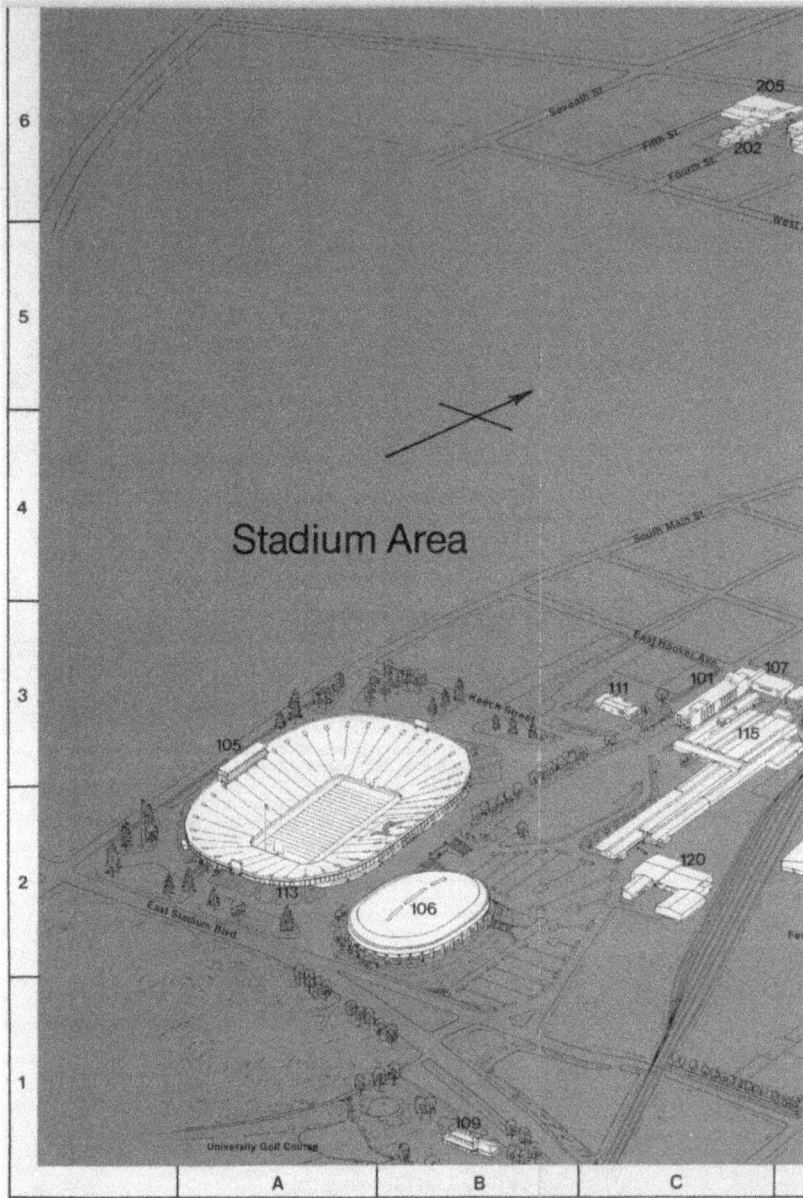

Stadium Area

	A	B	C
6			
5			
4			
3			
2			
1			

STADIUM AREA

101 Administrative Services Bldg., C-3
102 Athletic Administration Bldg., F-2
103 Fisher Baseball Stands, E-2
104 Coliseum, E-4
105 Communications Center, A-3
106 Crisler Arena, B-2
107 Data Services Center, C-3
108 Fletcher Hall, E-3
109 Golf Service Building, B-1
110 Intramural Sports Building, E-3
111 Mail Service Building, C-3
112 Matt Mann Pool, E-2
113 Michigan Stadium, A-2
114 Physical Properties Building, D-3
115 Plant Department, C-3
116 Revelli Hall, D-3

117 Sports Service Building, D-1
118 Tennis and Track Building, D-2
119 Ticket Office (Athletic), F-2
120 Transportation Services, C-2
121 Women's Athletic Building, E-2
122 Yost Ice Arena, E-2

OTHER LOCATIONS

201 Argus Building, D-6
202 Audio-Visual Education Center, C-6
203 Benz Building (Institute for the Study of Mental Retardation and Related Disabilities), F-6
204 109 E. Madison Building, E-4
205 Television Center, C-6

CENTRAL CAMPUS

1 Administration Building, G-4
2 Afroamerican and African Studies Center, H-3
3 Alumni Memorial Hall (Museum of Art), H-4
4 James B. Angell Hall, J-4
5 Angell Auditorium Unit, J-4
6 Architecture and Design Building, H-3
7 Betsy Barbour House, H-4
8 Margaret Bell Pool, M-3
9 Burton Memorial Tower, K-5
10 Business Administration Building, H-3
11 Business Administration Assembly Hall, H-3

D E F G

Central Campus

| H | J | K | L |

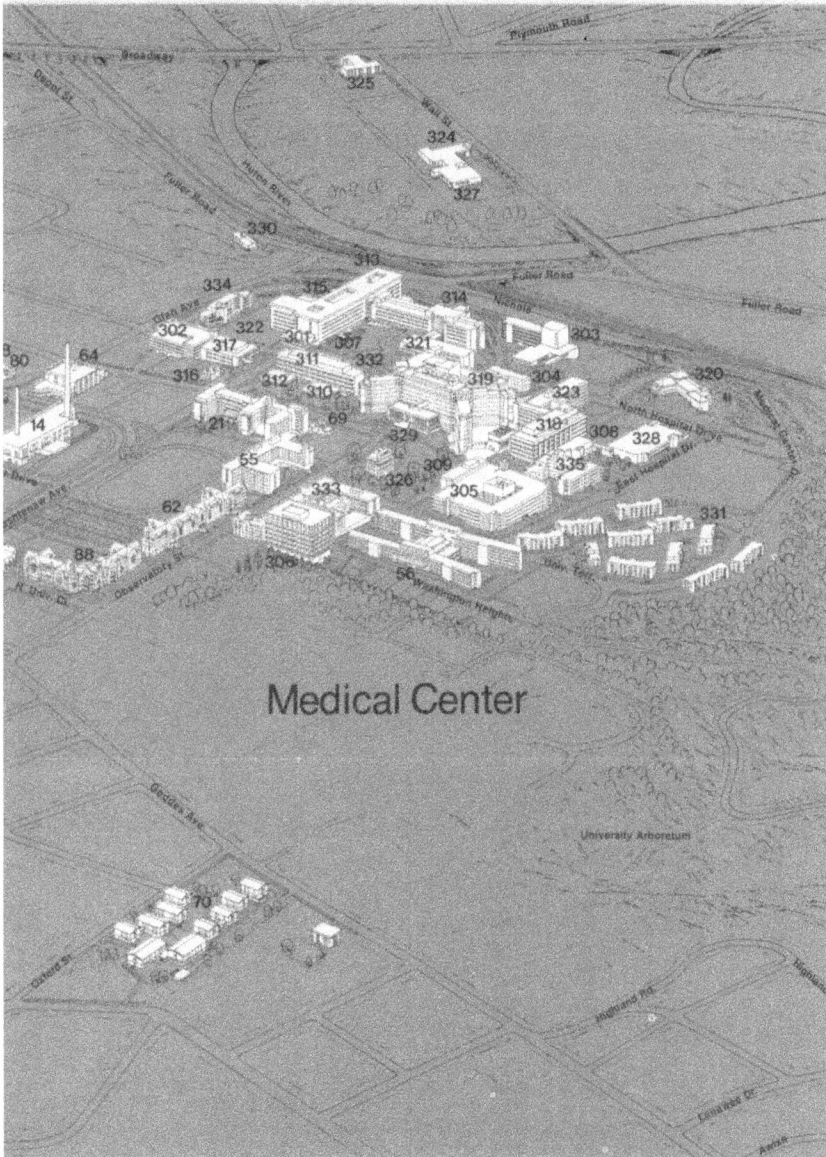

Medical Center

M | N | P | R | S

MEDICAL CENTER

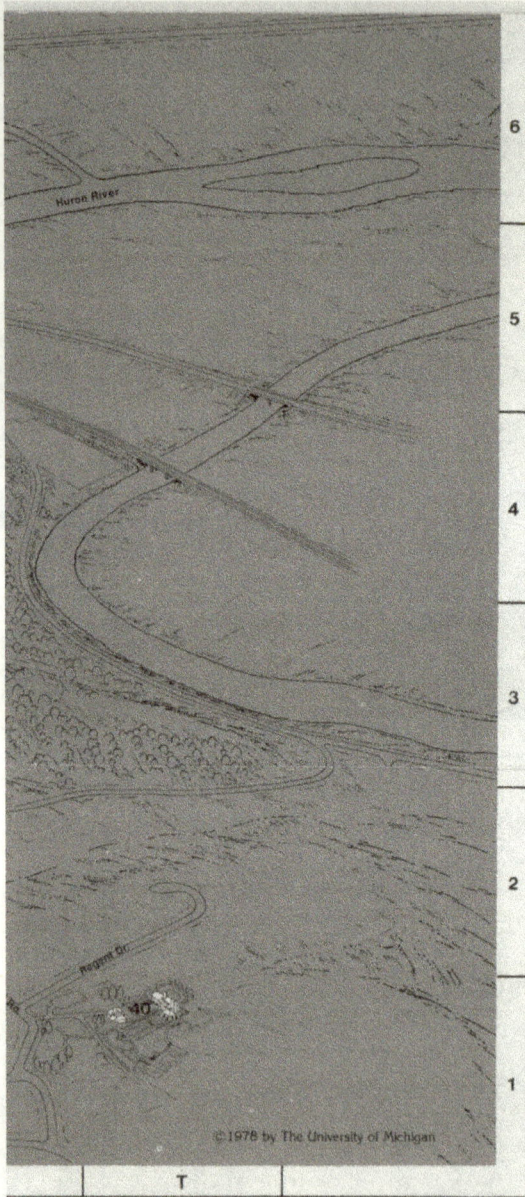

Huron River

Regent Dr.

6

5

4

3

2

1

T

© 1978 by The University of Michigan

317 Mental Health Research Institute,
    N-5
318 C.S. Mott Childrens Hospital, R-4
319 Neuropsychiatric Institute, P-5
320 North Outpatient Building, R-5
321 School of Nursing Building, P-5
322 School of Nursing Annex II, N-5
323 Outpatient Clinic, R-5
324 Parkview Medical, P-6
325 Riverview Building, P-6
326 Simpson Memorial Institute, P-4
327 Scott and Amy Prudden Turner
    Memorial Clinic, P-6
328 Towsley Center for Continuing
    Medical Education, R-4
329 University Hospital, P-4

330 University Hospital Education
    Center, N-5
331 University Terrace Apartments,
    R-4
332 Upjohn Center for Clinical
    Pharmacology, P-5
333 Henry F. Vaughan Public Health
    Building, P-4
334 Victor C. Vaughan House, N-5
335 Women's Hospital, R-4